Acknowledgements

My heartfelt thanks to our good friends Fred and Betty Hicks for their extreme patience and labor of love in the editing of this manuscript. We praise the Lord for you.

Contents

Introduction

God wants to move!

Early in my Christian walk, the Holy Spirit spoke to me one morning, 'Don't be sober with unbelief; be drunk with expectation.' One of the greatest lacks in the body of Christ is the lack of expectation. God is always willing to do more in our lives, but He won't move beyond our level of hunger and desire. The greatest commodity we possess as Christians is hunger for God! We must be diligent to maintain that hunger. In this book, I address ways the Holy Spirit moves and how we can see a greater demonstration of His power in our lives.

In order to see God do more, we must live with a continual demand on His presence. Countless people live in a 'business as usual' state. They live without a desire for and recognition of God – that He can do more. But God is waiting upon our level of desire and passion to increase. Putting a demand on His presence is an act of faith and belief. It is living with a tenacity toward God, recognizing His willingness to provide for our need.

The mistake many people make is living with an attitude of 'leaving it up to God.' However, from God's perspective, He is waiting on **us** to press in to His promises. He has already set a table, a smorgasbord of enormous proportions. But He cannot make us eat and partake.

There must not only be a posture of expectation, but a willingness on our part to submit our analytical minds to the flow of the Holy Spirit. It is the mind of man (not the devil) that aborts the work of the Spirit in our lives. When God speaks, He calls forth results that have nothing to do with natural circumstances.

> '... *who calls those things which do not exist as though they did.*'   (Romans 4:17)

Our reasoning mind becomes His enemy.

> '*Because the carnal* (natural) *mind is enmity* (hostility) *against God.*'   (Romans 8:7)

Therefore our puny brain is an abrasive to the Holy Spirit. God is the Author of our faith and frankly He doesn't respect our input when He declares what He is going to do. He hates unbelief, specifically when the mind scrutinizes what He is calling into existence. The analytical mind is the culprit that hinders the Holy Spirit, because the natural mind is an enemy (a hostile enemy) to the Spirit of God. For the body of Christ to experience total victory, the ultimate price must be paid. We must **yield** our analytical minds to Him. Jesus was crucified at Golgotha, which means the Place of the Skull (John 19:17). This is where we must ultimately be crucified – at the place of the skull. The brain has to be submitted and totally surrendered to the Holy Spirit.

In this book I give many examples of the power of the creative word of God. The Holy Spirit is always speaking (if we have ears to hear Him), and when He speaks to us His words are filled with creative power. The creative word of God is one of the most exciting aspects of the Christian life. There is no shortage of His miraculous power, and recognizing the prophetic utterances of the Spirit of God, catapults us into a whole new arena of knowing His power. Awesome things take place when we hear Him speak to us.

As we live a life of greater dependence on God, we recognize that maturity is far more than the lack of sinning, or being faithful in church attendance. Spiritual maturity can best be defined as when a believer begins to trust the witness of the Spirit in the inner man more than his physical senses.

As we dare to believe God and exert faith in our lives, we don't have the luxury of looking at the natural. This may be the greatest challenge for the believer. We all want to have our senses satisfied, as in the old adage, 'I'll believe it when I see it.' But we have to believe it **before** we see it. This simply means trusting the Holy Spirit. This is not meant to be difficult, but rather requires a decision to live a lifestyle of paying attention to the Holy Spirit. The Gospel is a Person. God has ordained that we live in continuous communion with Jesus Christ. **Jesus did not die to merely get us into heaven; He died to restore us into fellowship with God.** Therefore, we are not walking around in blind faith believing facts that have been taught us, but living a life of intimate communion and listening to the Holy Spirit.

The Holy Spirit is the Spirit of Truth. He will **never** lie or deceive us. That is why it is of utmost importance to always have an attitude and posture of **agreeing** with Him when He speaks. He will be faithful to watch over what He has spoken and bring it to pass.

Chapter 1

Come and Buy!

'And you who have no money, come buy and eat.'
(Isaiah 55:1)

When we walk into a retail store, a clerk will usually approach us with the standard question, 'May I help you?' Most often we give the standard response, 'No thank you, I'm just looking.'

Usually we are guilty of doing the same thing to the Lord. The Holy Spirit approaches us and broods over us, wanting to do something new for us, saying 'May I help you?' But by our actions we dismiss His invitation with an attitude that declares, 'No thank you, I'm just looking.'

When we search for the mind and will of God, we must have a posture that far exceeds looking. What does God require of us? God exhorts us to **buy** from Him!

> *'Ho! Everyone who thirsts, come to the waters; and you who have no money, come, **buy** and eat. Yes, come, **buy** wine and milk **without money** and **without price**.'*
> (Isaiah 55:1)

When we come before God in our individual prayer time, or when we come as a part of a group of worshippers, the Holy Spirit wants us to maintain one passion ... **to buy**! A great weakness among Christians is that of passivity toward God, and an unbelief in the willingness of God to manifest Himself to us.

For example, when we come to church, the Lord is in our midst, and He is approaching each individual saying, 'May I help you?' Because of unbelief or feelings of unworthiness, we often reply, 'No thank you, I'm just looking.' The Holy Spirit moves on to another person to ask the same question. He is looking for buyers!

The currency is hunger

God exhorts us to come and buy without money and without price. We don't need money as currency. The currency He requires is hunger. There is something about hunger that touches the heart of God. Jesus said,

> 'Blessed are those who hunger and thirst for righteousness, for they shall be filled.'   (Matthew 5:6)

It is hunger, not curiosity or interest, that moves the heart of God. Self-satisfaction and the lack of hunger, are what **tie** His hands.

> 'A **satisfied** soul loathes the honeycomb, but to a **hungry** soul every **bitter** thing is sweet.'   (Proverbs 27:7)

When someone is hungry, even the bitter thing is sweet. That which is bitter represents change. When there is true hunger, there is a willingness to let God work in us. Human nature resists, but the Holy Spirit always leads us to change into His purpose.

> 'And do not be conformed to this world, but be **transformed** by the renewing of your mind, that you may prove what is that good and acceptable and perfect will of God.'
> (Romans 12:2)

To someone who is not hungry for God there will be no desire to change. But when we are hungry, we want the will of God. We want to depart from self-satisfaction and be conformed into what He wants us to be.

Buying jewelry

When walking through a department store, it is hard to avoid the fine jewelry department. I always tell my wife, 'Eyes straight ahead please.' On the counter tops are arrays of earrings, watches, necklaces and bracelets that look attractive, but are priced very inexpensively. The store owners feel little risk of theft of this jewelry, as it has a relatively small value. However, underneath this 'surface' is a locked glass case filled with fine expensive jewelry. In order to touch and hold this jewelry you must ask the clerk to get a key and unlock the case. The clerk will oblige and usually let you see and handle one piece at a time. The store doesn't trust you, and refuses to be placed at risk of anyone stealing the items. You can become the owner of this jewelry, if you will consider the cost and are willing to pay the price.

Many of God's treasures are available, but they require a price. The Lord doesn't casually offer things of value to those who aren't hungry. But if you have desire, and 'hunger' for the greater treasures, He will make them available to you. Many enter God's presence with no hunger or anticipation, and therefore make no demands on Him. They are interested only to look with a casual eye at what is on the surface, which obviously requires little price (or effort) on their part.

In God's Kingdom, on the surface there are the things of God, such as a sense of His love, peace and joy. One cannot enter a worshipping church, or spend time in prayer without feeling the presence of God. But feeling a little peace, and tasting a little joy, or being lifted by the presence of God is far **different from buying** from Him.

Many people were bumping into Jesus the day when the woman who had the issue of blood touched Him. When Jesus questioned who had touched Him, Peter helpfully 'explained' to Jesus that many people were touching Him in the multitude that pressed against Him. But Jesus pointed out the difference. This woman had come to buy! Her hunger and determination were so great that she 'pulled' virtue out of Him, causing Him to say,

> *'Somebody touched Me, for I perceived power going out from Me.'*   (Luke 8:46)

It is one thing to 'brush against Him' or to feel His presence; but it is quite another to 'buy' from Him.

You can enter a church, for example, either as a spectator or as a shopper. Countless multitudes come into God's presence as 'just looking' and go away the same as they came. But God wants us to make a 'purchase' from Him each time we assemble, using the currency of our hunger and thirst. We can go before God putting a demand or draw on His presence, saying, 'Lord, I don't want to leave here the same way I came. I want something from you that I didn't have before. I have come to buy!' God will go out of His way to grant this desire. There is no limit to His storehouse and His resources.

> *'We shall be satisfied with the goodness of Your house, of Your holy temple. By awesome deeds in righteousness You will answer us, O God of our salvation, You who are the confidence of all the ends of the earth, and of the far-off seas.'*   (Psalm 65:5–7)

> *'You visit the earth and water it, You greatly enrich it;* **The river of God is full of water:** *You provide their grain, for so You have prepared it.'*   (Psalm 65:9)

If we come to God to buy, we will not be disappointed.

If you're hungry

If you're hungry you won't be looking for surface things when you come to church. You won't care about the appearance of the building, the shade of paint on the walls, or what the youth pastor looks like. No, you will be looking for the depth of the flow of the Holy Spirit. Our depth of hunger determines the depth of what we are looking for from God.

> *'Again, the kingdom of heaven is like treasure hidden in a field, which a man found and hid; and for joy over it he goes and sells all that he has and* **buys** *that field.'*
>   (Matthew 13:44)

Hunger is a great motivator. Hunger drives us to possess all that God has for us.

We determine our rate of growth

It seems that some people grow quickly in God, having experience after experience with Him. Others can hear the same teaching, be in the same atmosphere of worship and stay as shallow as a birdbath, spiritually. The difference is whether or not they have come to buy! Some have 'known' God for years, yet have never 'bought' anything from Him. They choose to stay only on a 'give me' level.

I have talked to seasoned salesmen and they have related to me how they can immediately recognize when someone is a serious buyer or someone just looking. Sharp salesmen often walk away from a customer who they recognize is just a tire-kicker. Don't you know that God must do the same thing? He knows if we are serious or if we are just playing a religious game, saying things we think He wants to hear, and merely loitering in the atmosphere of those who exhibit true passion for Him.

We need passion toward God. Passion in prayer. Passion in worship. Passion in believing.

I counsel thee to buy!

A few years ago I was ministering for a weekend at a gathering of a Christian organization. I arrived at the retreat grounds in mid-afternoon and began to pray for the meeting that evening. At one point I lay across the bed of my retreat room, and continued to pray. After several minutes, the Holy Spirit interrupted me and asked me a question. '**Do you know why they don't have the gold?**' I knew immediately that He was referring to the people to whom I would minister in a few hours. I responded to Him with a safe answer. 'No.' A few moments passed and He spoke again, giving me the answer to His question. '**They welcome Me, but they don't follow Me.**'

His words were sobering. No one fools God by outward appearances. He desires that we follow Him with an abandonment, not merely an enthusiastic welcome. He helped me understand what He meant about their lack of gold. These people had never purchased from Him the things of eternal value. They had never paid the price to follow on to know Him. Paul said,

> 'That I may know Him and the power of His resurrection, and the fellowship of His sufferings, being conformed to His death.'   (Philippians 3:10)

Some refuse to buy from God. They never ask Him to give them gold in their lives. Peter told us that we are *'partakers of the divine nature'* (2 Peter 1:4).

What to buy

When the Holy Spirit spoke to the church at Laodecia, He counseled them to buy. But first He described to them their condition.

> 'Because you say, "I am rich, have become wealthy, and have need of nothing" – and do you not know that you are wretched, miserable, poor, blind and naked.'
>   (Revelation 3:17)

These are strong words to believers (not lost sinners) who think they are in good shape – that they are wretched, miserable, poor, blind and naked. But then He counsels them to **buy**.

> 'I counsel you to **buy** from Me **gold** refined in the fire, that you may be rich.'   (Revelation 3:18)

Refined gold is from the process of the dealings of God, that make us rich in Him. It is easy to avoid Him and harden our hearts to His voice. There must be a continual, perpetual desire to follow Him and to **buy** gold. When we go through a hard place, it is a wonderful opportunity to buy. We can ask the Lord to reveal Himself to us and establish His divine nature (gold) into our lives.

Then He also counsels us to buy,

> '... *white garments, that you may be clothed, that the shame of your nakedness may not be revealed.'* (Revelation 3:18)

We must desire to be clothed in His righteousness only, not by the garments of our own good deeds as the result of our own agenda. Multitudes of people have little concern about eternity, and are not aware that presently they are all under the mercy of God. But once the heart stops, the mercy is cut off forever. Then there is only one question remaining as you go out into eternity. Are you clothed in the righteousness of Jesus Christ? Have you asked for forgiveness and let Him cleanse you with His blood? Nothing could be more tragic then going 'naked' into eternity. Paul said it rightly,

> '*For we know that if our earthly house, this tent, is destroyed, we have a building from God, a house not made with hands, eternal in the heavens. For in this we groan, earnestly desiring to be clothed with our habitation which is from heaven, if indeed, having been clothed, **we shall not be found naked.**'* (2 Corinthians 5:1–3)

Finally, He counsels us to buy eye salve,

> '... *and anoint your eyes with eye salve, that you may see.'* (Revelation 3:18)

The greatest need we have is spiritual sight, that we might see things from **His** perspective. From God's perspective the Laodecians were blind. But we can **daily** ask the Holy Spirit for eye salve, for Him to anoint our eyes to see through the Spirit and see what He wants us to see.

When we are not choosing to buy from God we not only are blind, but spiritually deaf, because we have tuned Him out. When we aren't hearing Him our heart becomes hardened.

> '*Today, if you will hear His voice, do not harden your hearts as in the rebellion.'* (Hebrews 3:15)

How to buy

We buy from God by aggressively putting a demand on His presence. Putting a demand is much like plugging an appliance into an electric outlet. Once plugged in, the appliance puts a draw or demand on the electrical supply. With God, we must plug into Him with desire and an attitude and passion that pulls virtue from His presence. For example, in prayer we can tell the Lord that we are wanting to buy from Him. We want His peace and joy manifested in a greater way in our lives. If we are praying for a specific need, such as someone we love who needs to come to Him, we can 'buy' with passion, by asking with expectation and desire. We can set our faith level to believe that this day, there will be results. After praying, we know we've 'bought' something from Him and the situation will never be the same. How not to buy would be to mumble passively some things we believe God wants to hear, or to pray a faithless prayer of 'whatever You want is okay with me,' instead of **seeing** what He has declared in His Word; that which is rightfully ours.

Another way to buy is to come to a meeting of God's people with an attitude to buy. We can put a demand on God's presence by telling the Lord we want to buy. We can say, 'Lord, I don't want to leave here like I came. I want something from you.' We can ask Him to heal us, speak to us, to let something be said that is a specific message to us.

It is not God's decision, it is ours

God always wants to move, but we have to make room for Him. In fact, I believe the Spirit of God leaves meetings of God's people 'frustrated' because He wanted to do more, but there was little expectation on the part of the people.

If we understand that God has already determined to move in our midst, then we will be less apt to follow our agenda so intently and, instead, have eyes and ears focused to behold what He is desiring to do. I firmly believe we often mishandle the anointing. Song leaders feel the anointing and sing too many songs. The Holy Spirit wants the people to break forth into free worship – singing in the Spirit and entering the

Holy of Holies – but **too many** songs quench the Spirit. Preachers often preach too long, instead of making room for the Spirit to move in other ways. Often the ego of the preacher feels what He has to say is too important and people become worn out and the Spirit is quenched. Even prayer can frustrate the Spirit of God, if people drone on and on and are insensitive to what the Holy Spirit might be prompting them to do.

The bottom line is that God wants to move – and if we will listen to His initiatives, He will speak life into the meeting and begin to perform creative acts according to His power.

Virgins who needed to buy

Jesus gave a parable likening the Kingdom of God to ten virgins who took their lamps and went out to meet the bridegroom. All ten are virgins, indicative of innocent or blood-washed Christians. Paul referred to chaste virgins as he wrote to Corinthian believers.

> *'For I have betrothed you to one husband, that I may present you as a chaste virgin to Christ.'* (2 Corinthians 11:2)

The most interesting part of the parable is that the five foolish virgins took no oil with them, while the five wise virgins took oil in their vessels with their lamps.

> *'Those who were foolish took their lamps and* **took no oil** *with them, but the* **wise took oil in their vessels** *with their lamps.'* (Matthew 25:3–4)

While the bridegroom delayed, they all slumbered and slept, but at midnight a cry came,

> *'Behold, the bridegroom is coming; go out to meet him!'* (Matthew 25:6)

All the virgins arose and trimmed their lamps, but the foolish had a problem – their oil was running out.

> *'And the foolish said to the wise, "Give us some of your oil, for our lamps are going out." But the wise answered, saying, "No, lest there should not be enough for us and you; but go rather to those who sell, and **buy** for yourselves." '*
>
> (Matthew 25:8–9)

When they returned from buying their oil, the door was shut. One thing for certain is we need to **buy** all we can from God while there is time. Why waste precious time God has given us to just spectate over His promises? We need to pursue God and buy. Most everyone is guilty of wasting time and even drifting from God at some point. How easy it is to waste a month, a year, or five years being distracted in some way. God is patient, but He has more time than we do. It is time to buy now.

Don't be sober with unbelief, be drunk with expectation

A number of years ago, when I was just beginning to understand the flow of the Holy Spirit, God spoke to me early one morning, 'Don't be sober with unbelief; be drunk with expectation.'

Our desire toward God should be that which makes us intoxicated and even delirious with desire.

Hannah was a perfect example of one who was drunk with desire. She was married to her husband, Elkanah, who also had a wife named Peninnah. Peninnah had children but Hannah had no children because God had closed her womb. But her husband greatly loved her and treated her preferentially.

> *'But to Hannah he would give a double portion, for he loved Hannah, although the Lord had closed her womb.'*
>
> (1 Samuel 1:5)

God has ways of provoking us to a higher level of desire. God used the other wife, Peninnah, to provoke Hannah.

> *'And her rival also provoked her severely to make her miserable, because the Lord had closed her womb.'*
>
> (1 Samuel 1:6)

Many times God uses an unlikely person to crowd us into faith and to intensify our desire. I'm sure Hannah didn't appreciate the chiding remarks from her rival, Peninnah, but God had a greater plan.

Her desire became so intense that she stopped eating. Her husband appealed to this reckless abandonment of desire.

> *'So it was, year by year, when she went up to the house of the Lord, that she provoked her; therefore she wept and did not eat. Then Elkanah her husband said to her, "Hannah, why do you weep? Why do you not eat? And why is your heart grieved? Am I not better to you than ten sons?"'*
>
> (1 Samuel 1:8)

Her husband made a good point. He blessed her and favored her as much as ten sons. We can identify with her in our relationship with God. Perhaps God has blessed you in such a way that is beyond reason, yet there is a deeper cry in your heart. **There is a great difference between being blessed and being fruitful.**

God had so convicted Hannah's heart through Peninnah, the instrument He used to provoke her, that she was at a point of desperation. In fact, her desperation was so immense that she was in great anguish.

> *'And she was in bitterness of soul, and prayed to the Lord and wept in anguish. Then she made a vow and said, "O Lord of hosts, if You will indeed look on the affliction of Your maid servant and remember me, and not forget Your maidservant, but will give Your maidervant a male child, then I **will give him to the Lord all the days of his life**, and no razor shall come upon his head."'*
>
> (1 Samuel 1:10–11)

Notice she was not praying selfishly, but rather with a desire **just to be the instrument** that God used to bring this child into the world. Her declaration was that she would give the child right back to the Lord.

Drunk with desire

When Eli the priest observed her as she wept and prayed in anguish, he didn't see her heart.

> *'And it happened, as she continued praying before the Lord, that Eli watched her mouth. Now Hannah spoke in her heart; only her lips moved, but her voice was not heard. Therefore Eil thought she was drunk.'*   (1 Samuel 1:12–13)

Then he rebuked her.

> *'So Eli said to her, "How long will you be drunk? Put away your wine from you!"'*   (1 Samuel 1:14)

Of course, Hannah wasn't drunk with wine, but she was **drunk with desire**!

> *'But Hannah answered and said, "No, my Lord, I am a woman of sorrowful spirit. I have drunk neither wine nor intoxicating drink, but have poured out my soul before the Lord. Do not consider your maidservant a wicked woman, for out of the abundance of my complaint and grief I have spoken until now."'*   (1 Samuel 1:15–16)

Her extreme desire toward the Lord to have a son made her appear drunk. To the natural mind she appeared intoxicated. Many times we will be misunderstood for being hungry for the Lord. Thank God that He sees our hearts and He **responds** to our longing and desperation. In fact, He is the one who brought us to that point! It didn't matter that Eli was unable to see her heart and accused her wrongly; God overruled his carnality and put a word in his mouth.

> *'Then Eli answered and said, "Go in peace, and the God of Israel **grant your petition** which you have asked of Him." And she said, "Let your maidservant find favor in your sight." So the woman went her way and ate, and her face was no longer sad.'*   (1 Samuel 1:17–18)

God moves according to our hunger and desire. He wants us to be filled with passion so much that He will provoke us to the point of desperation. Then we will approach Him with an attitude to 'buy' and we know what to ask for because we are praying according to His will and desire.

One who came to buy

The following is a classic example of someone who came to buy. It is such an awesome miracle, and it reveals God's extreme willingness to heal, although the answer seems 'slow' in coming. Joyce, from New Brunswick, Canada puts this in her own words.

Back in 1994 I was diagnosed with a health condition known as Sarcoidosis. Until that time I was a healthy 34-year-old woman with a great marriage and two wonderful little girls. Then my life changed dramatically. I became sick and no one seemed to be able to find out why. I was always short of breath and was experiencing constant swelling in my feet, ankles, and knees. Normal everyday activities such as walking became increasingly difficult. The swelling never went away and I never felt like I could get enough air. For a six-month period I underwent a very extensive amount of testing and was examined by more types of doctors than I knew existed. Many of these tests and examinations were at a hospital two hours from my home.

The first indication of what may have been happening with my body was a series of chest x-rays that showed black spots all through my lungs. When the doctor first showed the x-rays to my husband and me, I could not believe it was **my** lungs we were looking at. I had never smoked in my life and I just couldn't believe these pictures belonged to me. However, more and more advanced testing proved that my lungs really were the ones in the x-ray with black spots all through them. It was an extremely stressful time for the whole family. My children were really too young to fully understand what was happening but they were aware that life at home was very different.

It was decided that I would have to enter the hospital for a full week of more testing to try and better determine what was wrong. It was at this point in time that the doctor explained that it could be one of three areas. It was either Tuberculous, a form of Lymphoma or Sarcoidosis. Then I went home for a short time until one day my breathing became so labored that I had to be readmitted to the hospital and a lymph node biopsy was performed. Pastor Phil Lester and my husband took me to the hospital that day and I remember thinking that it was comforting to have Pastor Phil along but it was also a little unnerving to think that my husband did not want to go to the hospital without him. The biopsy confirmed that the condition afflicting my body was Sarcoidosis.

Sarcoidosis is a chronic condition of unknown origin and not a lot is known about it. Many people experience relief from anti-inflammatories and/or steroids. However, my body reacted negatively to different types of medications tried as treatments. I often felt desperate during this time as I longed for my life to return to normal. I wanted my life back and to be able to do things with my husband and children. The frustration of those days was indescribable.

Then one day at church, Pastor Phil announced that Reverend Steve Sampson was coming to the church for special meetings. Days later at a fellowship supper, the pastor's wife, Karen, asked if I were intending to come to the meetings. She said to be sure to come expecting a miracle, for if you came expecting nothing, that was what you would receive. I made a firm commitment in my mind right then and there that I was going to go to the meetings expecting a miracle. Not having been brought up in a fundamentalist church I was not sure what to think about healing services, but I was beyond desperate and was willing to try.

The first night of the meetings I was so excited I couldn't wait to get there. The first person that was prophesied over was my husband. It was wonderful to feel the spirit of God move in our lives and I couldn't wait till it was my turn. It didn't happen that night so I came to the meeting the next night full of anticipation. The meeting was great, but there was no healing message for me. That night after everyone in the family was in bed, I sat in the rocking chair in my kitchen and cried my eyes out. I talked to God for a long time pleading for a healing. The next morning we were getting ready for Sunday School and I just didn't think I could go. I wanted to, but I was feeling guilty for being so selfish, plus I was exhausted after staying up so late. In the end I did go that morning and while we were there my husband received another word from God through Steve Sampson. He looked right at me and said, 'There is something about you, but I don't know what it is.' Then he told me that he could see me singing God's praises but he just didn't know what it was he was sensing about me and he walked away. I remember sitting there thinking I can't sing and I'm going to be sick forever! I went home after church feeling somewhat discouraged; I really believed that I was going to receive a healing but it wasn't looking good to me at that time. I was also beating myself up for being so selfish and wanting this so bad.

That night was the last of the meetings and wonderful things were happening all around me. I was in a better mind set but still expecting so much when the meetings were being called to a close. Then, right as you were closing the meetings, you stopped and said that you were seeing someone that was having difficulty with lungs and breathing. I absolutely could not believe my ears, I sat right in my seat and could not move or speak. I listened again and when you asked if it fit anyone that was there, I just couldn't move. Then a couple of rows in front of me a good friend of ours turned around and very quietly said, 'Joyce, Joyce.' I remember it so clearly, but I also remember feeling like I was outside looking in and everything was in slow motion. Then when I finally raised my hand and you came back to where I was sitting, you looked right at me and asked if it were I and if it was a diagnosed condition. I said, 'Yes' and then you prayed over me. I was so excited and mentally drained that I could hardly stand up when it was time to go.

I knew that, beyond a shadow of a doubt, I was healed! The next day I left for a beach vacation with my girls and a friend and her daughter. This would have been impossible if God hadn't touched me. My husband wasn't sure we should go but I couldn't wait because I knew I was better. More doctor visits would assure me that this was true. I could hardly wait to have more x-rays taken and, when I did, my lungs were looking good, and then they just kept getting better. In April of this year I underwent a medical at the Lahey Hitchcock Clinic in Burlington, MA and the finding of the radiology results were 'The cardiomediastinal silhouette is normal. Lungs are clear. Conclusion: no active disease seen in the chest.' That statement may not be overly exciting to many people, but it was overwhelming to me, as it was just one more sign from the **Lord** that I have been given a second chance to live a healthy life and **sing His praises**, just like the anointed message was relayed to me.

Joyce Tozer, Miramichi, New Brunswick, Canada

Chapter 2

The Key of Expectation

- Those who expect nothing, give birth to nothing.

A pleasant-looking woman approached me one evening where I was speaking in Paducah, Kentucky. 'I can't wait to tell you what happened when you were here a year ago,' she told me. I eagerly listened, as she continued. 'That night as you ministered to the people, you gave a word from the Lord, saying "There is a woman around forty years old who has a heart condition."' She proceeded, 'Well, I was amazed that no one responded to receive prayer for that condition.' She beamed as she told me, 'I've had a heart condition for years, but I'm fifty-five.' Then with a big smile she said, 'When no one responded, I thought to myself, "**Shoot, I look forty,**" and so I stood and received prayer and embraced the creative word.'

She then explained how she had been on heart medicine since she was thirteen years old. That night she drove home and stopped at the bottom of the hill in front of her house. She ran all the way up the drive to the house. This would have been medically impossible a few hours earllier. It felt so good, she came back down and ran up the hill again. Then she went inside and woke up her husband (an unbeliever), to tell him what happened. He went back to sleep. (He had a spiritual heart problem.) That was Sunday night. On Tuesday, she went to her doctor who had treated her for years. He put her through extensive tests for the entire day. All the tests were conclusive. Her heart was in perfect condition.

He took her off all medication, and verified that she was completely healed.

Her expectation was on God. She received a complete healing of her heart, just because she dared to believe and say, 'I look forty.' I so appreciated her attitude and receptivity to God. God is so willing to manifest His word. I'm not sure if the word through me wasn't totally accurate (around forty years old), or if someone else didn't receive the word, and she chose to jump in and receive it. Either way, God rewards a heart full of expectation!

You need a key!

Have you ever locked yourself out of your car? It doesn't matter how nice a car it is; perhaps it is equipped with a powerful engine and leather interior and weighs two thousand pounds. Yet a small key that weighs less than an ounce, is needed to give you access to this powerful machine. You may live in a rambling house, yet if you ever lock yourself out, you still need that miniscule key to gain access to enjoy it.

No matter how big our God is, we still need a **key** to unlock His miraculous power in our lives.

Expectation is the key! It is the key to the miraculous and to releasing the power of God in our lives. The key of expectation opens the door to the supernatural flow of God. I like to say, 'Blessed are they who expect nothing, for they will not be disappointed.' So many live with a blasé attitude toward God, as if He isn't available or willing to do more. But David said, *'My expectation is from Him'* (Psalm 62:5).

The only thing that limits the power of God in our lives, is the lack of expectation we exhibit toward Him. God is always willing to do more. He is willing to do the miraculous in our lives, but few continually live with expectation.

Wrong expectation

When Naaman, the Syrian, arrived at the house of Elisha the prophet, he had wrong expectations. The prophet didn't come to greet him, but instead sent out a messenger (no doubt one who lacked a spiritual appearance) to give the message.

> *'Go and wash in the Jordan seven times, and your flesh shall be restored to you, and you shall be clean.'*   (2 Kings 5:10)

Rather than be thrilled to receive the word of the Lord, the warrior was angry. He declared those dangerous words, *'I said to myself...'*. He had preconceived ideas and limited expectations. In the vanity of his own mind, he developed a scenario that he wanted God to neatly perform. When the prophet didn't come out and wave his hand demanding the leprosy to disappear, Naaman became furious.

We can be guilty of doing the same thing. We limit God by having an extremely narrow expectation, telling God He can meet our need by only our specifications.

Naaman said,

> *'Indeed, I said to myself, "He will surely come out to me, and stand and call on the name of the Lord his God, and wave his hand over the place, and heal the leprosy."'*
> (2 Kings 5:11)

That is the way many of us believe. We think someone will show up and heal us and deliver us and we'll just watch it happen. But God **always sends us to the river!** The messenger told him he would get results if he would go to the River Jordan and dip seven times. God's promises always involve an effort on our part. (The woman with the issue of blood took great pain and effort to press through the crowd and touch the hem of His garment.)

Naaman was also angry about having to go to the River Jordan. He complained,

> *'Are not Abanah and the Pharpar, the rivers of Damascus, better than all the waters of Israel? Could I not wash in them and be clean?'*   (2 Kings 5:12)

We do the same thing. We are picky about the 'river' that God uses. We want to be healed or delivered at a respectable

'river' or the rivers at home, the familiar places, or at a
church with stained glass windows. Namaan complained
that the River Jordan wasn't as clean as the rivers at home. I
meditated on that. I wonder if that dirty Jordan represents
God's river that is dirty because so many needs of humanity
have been dipped in it.

Although Naaman was in a rage, his servants appealed to
him to obey because the prophet had instructed him to do
something simple and specific.

> '*So he went down and dipped seven times in the Jordan,*
> *according to the saying of the man of God; and his flesh*
> *was restored like the flesh of a little child, and he was clean.'*
> (2 Kings 5:14)

It seems that God will always require **us** to obey and make
the effort to **get into the river**. Human nature wants to
spectate and let someone else do it for us. But like Naaman,
we must take the plunge and make the effort to get into the
water. God will not pick us up and put us in it. He not only
had to get into the river, but the prophetic promise was that
he had to dip seven times. Seven represents completion or
perfection.

With each dip something gets buried

I formerly believed that nothing happened to Namaan until
the seventh dip. But now I know that something happened
to him on the **inside** each of the six times he dipped in
obedience to the word of the Lord. On the first dip, the spirit
of **pride** was submitted and buried in the river of God. Things
were happening on the **inside** of him. Flesh was being
washed away in the water before his affliction was cleansed
and healed. On the second dip, the spirit of human respect
(the fear of man) was submerged. By dip number three, an
attitude of cynicism and criticism was surrendered to God.
On dip four, he yielded up his unbelief. At dip five, his self-
reliance and independence were washed away. Dip six was a
once-and-for-all total abandonment to the will of God. By
then he didn't care if he was healed at all, for he was a free

man. . . . But on the seventh and final dip, he came up out of the water clean, with 'new' skin, like the flesh of a child.

What is expectation?

When my daughter, Brittani, was in the fourth grade, one day her class and the other fourth grade classes went on a field trip to visit the State capital. I volunteered to help the teachers and drive a car load of talkative fourth graders on the two hour trip. This is a Christian school and I wasn't surprised when, before getting into the caravan of cars and vans, one of the teachers insisted that we pray. So with children and parents standing in the parking lot with bowed heads, the teacher began to pray. In earnest, but yet in a mechanical way, she prayed for the safety of our travels and so forth. Then she pointed out to God (He wasn't aware) that the weather was cold and rainy, and simply asked God that if it somehow would be in His will (if not, that was okay too), that He would stop the rain long enough so we all could enjoy our picnic down by the river in Montgomery, Alabama.

I agreed with that prayer and assumed everyone else had also. Well, it rained the entire trip. When we reached the capital, we spent two hours touring the state congress and several other places of interest. Finally, it was time for lunch. Although there was still a steady rain, we piled into our vehicles and drove to a picnic area by the river. The sky was very gray, but the rain seemed to be lessening. We cautiously got out of the vehicles and made our way down the slope to the picnic area, each adult and child with a sack lunch in his hand. Amazingly, I watched as in the midst of the gray sky, the clouds pulled back, and the sun broke through. For twenty minutes or so, we all sat there eating sandwiches and chips, while most everyone was engrossed in quiet conversation. The sun brought a warmth to our chilled bodies. Slowly, people began to stand up, gather up the paper sacks and throw them in the trash. As we made our way back to our vehicles, I noticed the clouds forming back together, and soon the rain began to pour again.

Later, while in one of the capitol buildings, I commented to the teacher who had prayed previously. 'Boy, the Lord sure answered your prayer specifically.' She looked at me oddly. 'You know,' I continued, 'the rain stopped and the sun came out during the picnic.' Again she looked at me strangely and said, 'Yeah.' Disappointed, I approached some parents who also were chaperoning. I made a similar comment how God had stopped the rain, and received similar blank stares.

It made me wonder why God even honors our prayers, when they are prayed without **any** expectation, or **acknowledgment** when the prayer is answered.

After more than twenty-five years of ministry, I am convinced that the key of expectation is one of the most significant areas (and most under-used) in the life of the believer.

Expectation is hope. It is anticipation. It is coming before God with a total trust and confidence in His ability to manifest something on our behalf.

When a mother-to-be is expecting, she anticipates seeing the manifestation of a baby in her arms. We can live this way, knowing that the Holy Spirit is willing to **birth** all the promises of God in our lives.

No mother is surprised when a baby is born!

God's way of manifesting Himself to us is that He impregnates us with a promise. Just as in the natural, when a woman conceives, she has no proof (except perhaps vomiting) that there is a baby on the way. A visit to the doctor confirms that there is indeed a baby. But what if someone said to her, 'Show me the baby!' She would have to say, 'I can't show it to you, but there is a baby inside of me.' There may be a comment, 'Well, I don't believe it because I can't see it or hear it.'

But the baby is very much a reality. Although it hasn't reached the point of manifestation, it is very much a living person.

God's promises are also a reality. I don't mean just randomly picking a scripture verse, but when the Holy Spirit communicates to you that He is indeed going to manifest a promise in your life. Once He gives you that oracle, whether through a witness of the Spirit, a dream, a specific scripture that leaps off the page, a vision, or by a prophetic word through someone, it is a fact. You are pregnant with that word. At that point it is a reality, although you may have to walk through a time period before your physical senses can enjoy the manifestation.

That is why no woman is surprised the day she gives birth. The baby has been a reality for months! In a sense, the baby is 'old news'. The day of delivery is simply the full manifestation of what has already been a reality.

Business as usual

Countless people live in a 'business as usual' state. They live without a desire for or recognition of God – that He can do more. But God is waiting upon our level of desire to rise.

For example, every time Israel cried out to God, He heard their cry and wrought deliverance for them. We need to learn to live with a passionate desire to experience more.

A small child may whine and cry all day. The mother quickly tunes out a lot of moans and whining. But at times there will be a different cry which sends the mother running because she recognizes his sincerity. God waits for our cries to Him to carry more passion and desire. He hears a moan and tolerates our whine, but a cry of desperation and expectation causes Him to attend to us.

Jesus said,

> *'Blessed are they who hunger and thirst for righteousness, for they shall be filled.'* (Matthew 5:6)

God responds to hunger! The greatest commodity we possess is hunger. As long as we are hungry, God will show us more and more. But how tragic it is when our hunger has waned and our expectation lessens.

Don't window shop

Many men don't like to shop. When they do, it is like a hunting trip. They quickly make their way through the store, find the size of shirt they need, bag it, and are ready to leave the mall. Most women, on the other hand, love to shop, not necessarily to buy anything in particular, but just to look and admire. Women enjoy window shopping, just to see what is for sale, and to admire and dream. But most men perceive this as a waste of time.

The church is full of window shoppers. They are not present in order to put a demand on God, but merely to look. But God wants us to live with expectation at all times, especially when we come to church. He wants us to come with expectation that will **pull** virtue from His person. The weakest quality of the church is a lack of a sense of worthiness, so we inevitably pray ignorantly, with an anaemic appeal, 'If it be thy will.' People think it is up to God what He manifests in our life, but God is **limited** by our level of passion and desire. He won't intrude upon our low level of faith. Like a gentleman, He waits for our passion to increase. He gets enthused when we get enthused.

God does not disappoint

When people come with expectation, it is amazing what the Holy Spirit will do. One evening in Kentucky as I was preaching, I suddenly felt a strong unction to pray for a certain woman in the crowd. The Holy Spirit led me to pray specifically, showing me that she had a particular need in her physical body. I spoke what God told me – that He was healing her body. I knew I had obeyed God, and she seemed overwhelmed to say the least. Immediately after the meeting, the pastor's wife came to me crying with such gratitude to the Lord. She told me how, during the entire meeting, she had prayed and prayed that the Lord would have something personal to say to this specific lady, because she had never been in a Christian meeting where the gifts of the Holy Spirit were in operation. I immediately knew that the **only** reason God had given me the directive to approach this certain lady out of the entire crowd, was because this pastor's wife had prayed with expectation and desire.

One night in a small town in Indiana, I had a similar experience. As I preached, the Holy Spirit spoke to me someone's last name. When I asked the group gathered whose name it was, a nine-year-old boy raised his hand. I went to him and with his permission, prayed for him on the spot. The Holy Spirit spoke clearly to this young man about his life. His mother told me later how she had been sitting there in fervent prayer and great expectation that God would speak to her son, as their home was broken and his mind was so confused. God clearly answered her prayer as she prayed and put a demand on God, and her son will never forget how much God cares for him.

Lack of expectation

When we hear the name of Jesus, it is easy to conceive of Him being able to do anything. But there was a situation where He **could not** perform miracles. It happened to take place at His home town of Nazareth.

His power was extremely limited by the gross lack of expectation of the 'locals.' They couldn't draw from His presence because of their carnality.

> *'And many hearing Him were astonished, saying, 'Where did this Man get these things? And what wisdom is this which is given to Him, that such mighty works are performed by His hands! Is this not the carpenter, the Son of Mary, and brother of James, Joses, Judas, and Simon? And are not His sisters here with us?'' So they were offended at Him.'*
>
> (Mark 6:2–3)

Their familiarity with the natural side of Jesus, reduced their expectation to nothing.

Jesus addressed this very point.

> *'A prophet is not without honor except in his own country, among his own relatives, and in his own house.'* (Mark 6:4)

Then the reality of the shame of what they missed is recorded.

> *'Now **He could do no mighty work there**, except that He laid His hands on a few sick people and healed them. And*

He marveled because of their unbelief. Then He went about
the villages in a circuit, teaching.'   (Mark 6:6)

One of the most graphic Scriptures indicating lack of
expectation is,

'And no one, having drunk old wine, immediately desires
*new; for he says, "**The old is better**."'*   (Luke 5:39)

Another is,

*'A **satisfied soul** loathes the honeycomb, but to a **hungry***
***soul**, every bitter thing is sweet.'*   (Proverbs 27:7)

Probably one of the most precious commodities we possess
as Christians is that of spiritual hunger. Tragically, people
often lose their hunger, and it is usually because God has
blessed them and they've become satisfied. We must always
desire and expect **more** from God.

Our expectation level is weak

When my wife and I were pastors, one evening we invited a
guest speaker to tell his testimony of how he had been healed
in a Kathryn Kulhman meeting. Many mind-boggling miracles had taken place in the meetings of this mighty woman
of God. He related to us how he had been diagnosed with
terminal cancer and doctors could do nothing for him. As a
last resort, he decided to attend a Kathryn Kulhman service,
as he had heard about this 'faith-healer's' mighty results.

When he arrived at the meeting he was seated in the
balcony, and listened as the song leader led the crowd in
several choruses. Then Miss Kuhlman began to preach. After
preaching for a while, she suddenly stopped and pointed up
into the balcony where this man sat. 'Someone in this
section of the balcony in the third row has just been healed
of cancer,' she proclaimed. He related how he just sat there.
She preached a little longer. Again she stopped, pointed once
more toward him in the balcony and gave the same proclamation, 'Someone right over here in the balcony in the third

row has just been healed of cancer.' Still he sat there. She preached again and soon stopped and for the third time said, 'Someone in the balcony has been healed of cancer. You need to come down here right now.' Still he didn't move, but an usher approached him and said, 'Sir, I believe she is talking about you and God has healed you of cancer.' He told us how he accompanied the usher to the stage and how Miss Kuhlman interviewed him and prayed for him. By the change in his body, it was obvious he was healed by the power of God. Since that miraculous moment he has given his testimony all over America.

What a lack of expectation! Although he **came** to be healed of cancer, when Miss Kuhlman pointed at him, identified exactly where he was seated and declared that he was healed of cancer, he just sat there. I believe that is how strongly we are imbedded in unbelief. Although God is willing, we are numb with unbelief and anaemic in our expectation.

Several years ago I was ministering at a conference in New York. After preaching, I had a word from the Lord that I delivered to the crowd. 'There is someone here, who is fifty-three-years old who needs a healing. If you come forward for prayer, God will heal you.' No one responded. I waited patiently and then moved onto something else. But the following day, I was approached in the hotel lobby where I was staying, by a pastor and his wife who had driven a thousand miles to be in the conference. The pastor's wife apologized to me saying, 'Steve, I'm fifty-three-years old and am in desperate need of healing. But when you spoke that word last night about a person fifty-three that God wanted to heal, I just froze.' We stood there in the lobby and prayed for her, and hopefully she received her healing. I could not understand why she 'froze', but I do believe her slow response reveals how much we limit God by not living with expectation. Pride and timidity can rob us from receiving what God has in store for us.

Come as a child

The most difficult requirement for most of us is to come as a child. This doesn't mesh with the analytical and proud mind.

We love to analyze and reason our way, reducing God to the level of our intellect. But being humble isn't an option to choose; it is a command.

> '...*Unless you are converted and become as little children, you will by no means enter the kingdom of heaven. Therefore, whoever humbles himself as this little child is the greatest in the kingdom of heaven.*'   (Matthew 18:4–5)

Childlikeness has nothing to do with age or experience. It is a quality we need to maintain our entire life, in order to receive from our loving Father.

Expectation pulls virtue from God

Living with expectation is a posture that places a demand on the presence of God. When an appliance is plugged in, it pulls the current out of the electrical flow causing it to operate. For example, the room you are occupying right now is full of power, although you may feel no sensation or see or hear anything. There are no doubt several electrical outlets around you. But nothing will happen until you first plug in an appliance. By plugging it in, you put a 'demand' on the power supply. Although the power has always been available, nothing happens until you utilize the power source available.

If we don't think there is power in the room we occupy because there is no noise or sensation of power, I challenge you to take a paper clip and insert in into the receptacle in the wall. You'll notice there is 'power', as sparks fly and your body shakes!

We live toward God the same way. God is available to move, whether or not there is any perception or sense of power felt. The Lord is present in the room you are occupying right now, but there has to be an aggressive posture to plug into Him. He is willing to manifest Himself – but are we full of expectation that will put a demand on His power? How much greater is the opportunity when the body of Christ gathers together! We should always come to church or to a gathering to place a demand (through our expectation) on His presence. We can say, 'Lord, I'm not here to window shop, I'm here to receive from You!' He will manifest Himself through healing, encouragement, deliverance and in many other ways.

Naturally, the leadership needs to have the same attitude – that the Holy Spirit is willing to move, and to be open to Him as He desires to flow out to the people and to meet various needs. The highest priority of those in leadership must be a continual openness to the mind and will of the Holy Spirit.

Chapter 3

Living by Inside Information

'Who told you that you were naked?' (Genesis 3:11)

'Don't be afraid of bad news.' My wife heard the Lord speak these words to her one morning while she was in prayer. Less than six hours later we received a phone call from a friend involved in litigation with a serious lawsuit against him. We had been concerned about our friend who was an executive with a large corporation. We knew he wasn't guilty, and the charges against him were ridiculous. In fact, he is a devout Christian, and one of the most righteous and pure people we know. For weeks, we along with other believers, had prayed fervently for him. Among all who prayed, living in various parts of the country, there was a general consensus that God had heard and the situation was going to have a good outcome.

When we received the call from our friend, he was very distressed, telling us that the suit had gone against him, and involved an enormous settlement that he would be forced to pay from his own personal resources. It was so puzzling to us, knowing that all indications from the Spirit of God were that it was going to be okay. My wife encouraged him with the word she had heard from the Lord hours earlier, 'Don't be afraid of bad news.'

Within twenty-four hours, the president of the firm contacted him with good news. The president relayed that because of his excellent work record, the firm was going to pay the huge fine in his behalf. Although this wasn't how we thought the situation would turn out, we all rejoiced at the faithfulness of God. When we had first received the 'bad news' we couldn't believe it, as a number of us had felt we had heard the Lord clearly. But the Holy Spirit had also said, 'Don't be afraid of bad news' which was the inside information that came right out of heaven.

When God talks to us He gives us 'inside information', namely, insights that are hidden and are not known to the natural mind of man. This is the way Christians are to live – by information that the Holy Spirit supplies. What my wife heard that day was the Holy Spirit giving inside information. The world is full of information that leads to fear and distortion. But God knows the end from the beginning and He cannot lie. He will always tell us the truth.

This is one exciting aspect of being a believer. We don't have to heed any voices, except the voice of the Lord. His voice leads us and protects us from danger and calamity.

Who told you that you were naked?

When Eve, along with her husband Adam, succumbed to eating the fruit of the tree of the knowledge of good and evil, they hid themselves from the presence of the Lord. When God confronted them, Adam explained,

> *'I heard Your voice in the garden, and I was afraid because I was naked; and I hid myself.'* (Genesis 3:10)

Then God said,

> **'Who told you that you were naked?'** (Genesis 3:11)

In other words, God was questioning Adam's **source** of information. God's question clearly implies that we do not need to accept (or live by) any information that doesn't come from Him. Adam and Eve had received the wrong information – namely information that wasn't given to them by the Holy Spirit, but by their own senses. All information that does not come from the Holy Spirit is **outside information**.

The good news of the gospel is that the believer is only

responsible to live by inside information – information that the Holy Spirit gives us.

How many times have most of us said, 'I'm depressed' or 'I'm discouraged.' Or, 'I feel like a failure.' Or 'I feel sick and I'm getting worse.' But the Holy Spirit is tapping us on the shoulder saying, 'I beg your pardon, **where did you get that information? That information did not come from Me.**' It is astonishing **how much** of our lives we live by outside information we gather from circumstances, or the media, or through listening to the opinions and whims of people.

Forced to trust inside information

Whoever has children has most likely experienced a similar gut-wrenching scenario at one time as the following.

When my daughter, Brittani, was five-years-old, I took her and her older brother, David, to a water park for a day. David went off to the thrilling water slides with a friend, and I took her to a portion of the park designated for small children. Never had I ever seen such a large group of tiny tots in one setting. They all seemed to be in awe of the various slides, towers, pools, water gadgets, and a huge river shaped area that seemed to go on forever. As I looked out at these hundreds of children, I thought to myself what a great dad I was to treat my daughter to a day's worth of such fun.

As I bent down to speak to her, however, she was gone. I quickly scanned over the multitude of children, remembering the bow her mother had put in her hair that morning, and frantically searched for any sign of it. I could feel my heart sinking when I could not locate her anywhere. I looked for at least thirty minutes, praying fervently. Finally, prayer wasn't enough. I had to **look** into my inner man, and 'see' what God was saying. I needed **inside information**, and I needed it immediately, because there was nothing to give comfort to my natural eyes. When I 'looked' into my inner man, there was great peace, and I was flooded with the assurance that our daughter was okay. But where was she? Soon I could feel the panic creeping back, and I again had to consult the Holy Spirit. Again I was flooded with **peace** (inside information).

I thought about calling my wife at home, but I quickly disregarded that idea, for I knew she would 'kill' me and no doubt enter into her own panic.

At this point I desperately approached a lifeguard. 'I can't locate my five-year-old girl anywhere,' I told him. He was unmoved, and glibly stated, 'Oh, she'll show up.' For a second I had to deal with hatred toward him, but there was no time for that. I continued to look, walking the entire circumference of the play area. Every few minutes, feeling the sinking panic, I repeatedly 'looked' to the Holy Spirit in my inner man, grasping that peace each time.

Finally, I was getting so tired and frustrated not knowing what else to do. Exasperated, I knelt down, and there was Brittani, standing next to me. 'Where have you been?' I asked. 'I've been watching you,' she replied. She pointed to a huge platform of water toys she had been playing on, watching my movements the entire time.

During the entire scenario, my senses had **nothing** to go on. But the 'inside information' from the Holy Spirit had been accurate. She was indeed safe. We can always trust the Holy Spirit's guidance no matter what our senses dictate.

God doesn't lie

A number of years ago my wife and I were speaking for three days at a church in New Jersey. It was a wonderful time and the Spirit flowed in our midst. On the last night of the meetings, toward the end, the Holy Spirit spoke to one of us that there was a family who had a baby with a heart problem. We stood in awkward silence waiting for the person with this sickly baby to claim it so we could agree in prayer with them. But no one responded. We were notably puzzled when no one acknowledged the word, but continued with the meeting. The following morning we flew home.

A few days later, the pastor called me. He was excited. 'I couldn't wait to tell you what happened.' He said. 'Do you remember Lisa, the girl on the worship team?' I acknowledged that I did indeed remember her as she was very pregnant, obviously due at any time. 'Well,' he continued, 'the next day after you left, she went into labor and she and her husband made haste getting to the hospital. Soon their baby was born, but shortly after, a team of doctors came into their room with bad news. They gave her the sobering report, "Your baby has a serious heart problem and won't live more than twenty-four hours." '

Soon the pastor, along with many people from the church, gathered in the room to comfort the grieving parents. After hours of this depressing, unbelieving ritual, the pastor told me, it suddenly hit him. 'Hey,' (he addressed everyone present in the room) 'do you remember the word the Lord spoke on Sunday night, about a baby with a heart condition being healed?' They all nodded in agreement. 'This is the baby the Holy Spirit was talking about!' he excitedly exclaimed. They all began to rejoice and praise God fervently that the Lord had foreknowledge of this problem, and had already promised that His hand was moving in the creative realm.

The following morning the same team of doctors came into the room, saying, 'We don't understand this, but your baby will not die. In fact, your baby's heart is perfectly normal.'

This occurrence took place several years ago, and this precious boy has not had health problems of any kind since his birth. Thank God for the Holy Spirit who is never caught off guard and who gives us 'inside information' daily.

God doesn't change His mind

When the children of Israel had come out of Egypt, God hardened the heart of Pharaoh and he and his entire army were in pursuit. The children of Israel were trapped. Surrounded by mountains on both sides, the Red Sea before them and Pharaoh and his army fast approaching, they had no place to go. So they did the obvious thing: they began to gripe and complain and accuse Moses. They easily accepted the **outside information** their senses told them. But God hadn't changed His mind! Although the circumstances had seemingly changed, God still intended to keep His promise, which was to totally deliver them from the Egyptian bondage. Moses knew that God hadn't changed His mind and exhorted the people to believe.

> *'Do not be afraid. Stand still, and see the salvation of the Lord, which He will accomplish for you today. For the Egyptians whom you see today, you shall see again no more forever. The Lord will fight for you and you shall hold your peace.'* (Exodus 14:13–14)

Then God talked to Moses,

> *'Why do you cry to Me? Tell the children of Israel to go forward.'* (Exodus 14:15)

This sounds like God was being hard on Moses, but in essence, God was telling Moses (who obviously had been crying out to God) to stop asking and start moving on what he believed. Circumstances had drastically changed, but the mind of God had not.

As Moses stretched forth his rod, acting on inside information, the waters parted and they proceeded across.

The definition of maturity

Maturity is far more than the lack of sinning, or being faithful in Bible reading, and church attendance. Spiritual maturity can best be defined as when a believer begins to trust the witness of the Spirit in the inner man **more than his physical senses**.

How refreshing it is to encounter a believer who has reached the point of placing no confidence in his circumstances, or the information his senses give him, but is trusting in the 'inside information' of the Holy Spirit. Now that I've walked with God for a long season, it seems so obvious to me that this principle is one that is close to the heart of God. When His people are led by the Spirit, they are declared the sons of God (Romans 8:14). God also exhorts us,

> *'Trust in the Lord with all your heart* (not brain) *and lean not upon your own understanding. In all your ways acknowledge Him* (not your opinion) *and He shall direct your paths.'* (Proverbs 3:5–6)

God has ordained that we walk in the Spirit and listen to the Spirit, which is living by inside information. As Christians, we are only obligated to live by and act upon information that issues from the Holy Spirit within. His voice (inside informa- tion) supersedes and overrules all other sources or advice. Stockbrokers get in trouble if they engage in insider trading, which is buying and selling with knowledge or information that they didn't obtain legally. But as Christians, our way of life is to live by this inside information – and as we act upon it we will have success, and avoid a slew of troubles.

No luxury

As we dare to believe God and exert faith in our lives, **we don't have the luxury of looking at the natural**. This may be the greatest challenge for the believer. We all want to have our senses satisfied, as in the old adage, 'I'll believe it when I see it.' But we have to believe it **before** we see it. This simply means **trusting the Holy Spirit**. This is not meant to be difficult, but rather requires a decision to live a life style of paying attention to the Holy Spirit. The Gospel is a Person. It is a relationship that God has ordained that we live in continuous communion with Jesus Christ. **Jesus did not die to merely get us into heaven; He died to restore us to fellowship with God**. Therefore, we are not walking around in blind faith believing facts that have been taught us – but listening to a Person.

As we purpose to serve God, we live by inside information, not outside information. Christians have the awesome privi- lege of being privy to information that the Holy Spirit gives us – daily. In every situation, we have to be open to hear the inside information that the Holy Spirit freely gives.

One of the greatest lessons I've learned is not to demand God to act in a spectacular manner. For many, the super- natural is eclipsed because they are wrongly anticipating the spectacular. The Holy Spirit is always talking, and He is more than willing to talk to any one of us. We have to recognize that He is speaking to our spirit man and not to our brains. So few seem to understand this, and quickly rely on the logic of reasoning rather than the voice of the Lord.

A good example of this was when a friend of mine was injured on the job. He worked at a rock-crushing plant, and one day a vat of lime blew up in his face. Medical aid was administered, and the doctor informed him his eye was not permanently damaged, but he would still have to put a patch over it for several weeks. My friend, who was in his early sixties, told me how, as soon as the patch was placed on his eye, he began experiencing tormenting fear of having a heart attack. He battled this fear for days, while he was recovering at home.

One evening his daughter asked him to attend a meeting with her on the other side of Kansas City where an evangelist from New Zealand was speaking. He agreed to go with her, as he was bored sitting home every day. After the minister spoke for a while, he began to minister prophetically to various individuals in the audience. Feeling rather cynical, my friend thought to himself, 'I know what will happen. When he sees this patch on my eye, he'll call me forward and pray for my eye.' Several minutes later, just as he had 'thought', the evangelist called him out and asked him to come to the front. He went forward and stood in front of the minister. The man looked him straight in the eye and said, 'The Lord told me to tell you there is nothing wrong with your heart.' He never mentioned his eye.

Obviously, this evangelist had learned not to trust outside information but to totally rely on the mind of the Holy Spirit.

When you're old

Jesus prophesied to Peter a very specific word,

> 'Most assuredly, I say to you, when you were younger, you girded yourself and walked where you wished; **but when you are old**, you will stretch out your hands, and another will gird you and carry you where you do not wish.'
>
> (John 21:18)

Months later, Peter was in a predicament. Herod had James, John's brother, killed. When he gained approval with the Jews, he had Peter arrested and put in prison.

> *'So when he had arrested him, he put him in prison, and delivered him to four squads of soldiers to keep him, intending to bring him before the people after Passover.'*
> (Acts 12:4)

So Peter was in prison, knowing full well what had happened to his peer, James. The whole church was praying.

> *'But constant prayer was offered to God for him by the church.'* (Acts 12:5)

However, the Scriptures make such an interesting claim.

> *'And when Herod was about to bring him out, **that night Peter was sleeping**, bound with two chains between two soldiers; and the guards before the door were keeping the prison.'* (Acts 12:6)

I question how Peter could be sleeping, knowing that there were heavy odds of his being executed the following morning. No doubt, the guards had chided him with that fact when they threw him in prison. But Peter obviously **held fast to** the prophetic word that Jesus had spoken to him, *'when you are old, you will stretch out your hands, and another will gird you and carry you where you do not wish.'*

Peter had to recognize that, since Jesus had referred to things happening when he was old, that he wasn't anywhere near old. Having this 'inside information' Peter was able to sleep. And so deep was his sleep that an angel had to strike him on the side to get him to wake up.

> *'Now behold, an angel of the Lord stood by him, and a light shone in the prison; and he struck Peter on the side and raised him up, saying, "Arise quickly!" And his chains fell off his hands.'* (Acts 12:7)

There are more with us than with them

The king of Syria sent an army to seize Elisha, because Elisha 'by the Spirit' continued to reveal his battle plans.

> *'Therefore he sent horses and chariots and a great army there, and they came by night and surrounded the city.'*
> (2 Kings 6:14)

His servant was only seeing outside information.

> *'And when the servant of the man of God arose early and went out, there was an army, surrounding the city with horses and chariots. And his servant said to him, "Alas, my master! What shall we do?"'* (2 Kings 6:15)

The natural eyes only serve to give us outside information. But the eyes of the Spirit furnish inside information.

So the prophet declared the real truth, which was inside information,

> **'Do not fear, for those who are with us are more than those who are with them.'** (2 Kings 6:16)

Then he prayed for the servant's eyes to be opened (spiritually),

> *'"Lord, I pray, open his eyes that he may see." Then the Lord opened the eyes of the young man, and he saw. And behold, the mountain was full of horses and chariots of fire all around Elisha.'* (2 Kings 6:17)

What is exciting here is that nothing had changed! All was well. The only change was that the servant's eyes were opened to see the right information. Sometimes we demand God to bring change, but what we really need is for God to open our eyes so we see things as He sees them.

God cannot lie

I always encourage myself with the truth that God cannot lie. When He gives you and me 'inside information' it will come true. I was the speaker at a church in Ohio last year. The Holy Spirit spoke as I was ministering to the people that someone was very close to losing a long-held secure job. A man in his forties raised his hand, acknowledging that this was indeed the situation he was in. I encouraged him in the Lord with the fact that the Holy Spirit had revealed this knowledge; that since God was in control, he was not to be concerned as his job was secure. Then we all prayed and thanked God. However, in the natural his situation seemed utterly hopeless. The huge corporation where he had worked for over twenty years was going out of business. This man had to choose to believe the word of the Lord. But within a few weeks, the oil company where he was employed, was bought out by another oil conglomerate (much to the surprise of the entire community) and his job was secure. The Holy Spirit doesn't lie.

God ignores circumstances

It always amazes me the way God seems to forget to inform us of the seemingly most significant facts of a situation. It seems as though God occasionally suffers from temporary amnesia. For example, when He had Moses send twelve spies into Canaan to check it out, He gives them no details of problems they might encounter.

> ' "Go up this way into the South, and go up to the mountains, and **see what the land is like**; whether the people who dwell in it are strong or weak, few or many; whether the land they dwell in is good or bad; whether the cities they inhabit are like camps or strongholds; whether the land is rich or poor, and whether there are forests there or not. Be of good courage. And bring some of the fruit of the land." Now the time was the season of the first ripe grapes.'
>
> (Numbers 13:17–20)

It is so interesting that He does not warn them that there are huge giants in the land. Why? Because God doesn't care about giants or any other extraneous circumstances. He 'thinks' He is still in control and the promise is still valid, even though the land is full of giants.

When the spies returned, they were overwhelmed by the observation they had made of the giants.

*'We went to the land where you sent us. It truly flows with milk and honey, and this is its fruit. **Nevertheless the people who dwell in the land are strong; the cities are fortified and very large; moreover we saw the descendants of Anak there.'*** (Numbers 13:27–28)

It is exactly the same when the Holy Spirit talks to you and me. As far as God was concerned, the land belonged to them. The giants would have to go. In **all** of God's promises, we have to deal with 'giants' who oppose us possessing what God has.

God's way is to tell you the **outcome** of the situation or trial. He may tell you that you are coming into a season of prosperity; yet for a duration you have the worst season of financial struggle you've ever had. However, following the trial, you then experience the prosperity that He promised.

As believers, we learn that **anything** God says is inside information and He can be trusted. Yes, there are obstacles and hurdles before the outcome, but He doesn't lie. I like to put it this way; you must 'see it' (in the spiritual realm) before you actually see it manifested in the natural realm. If you'll see it before you see it, then you'll see it!

There will always be the opportunity to return

The devil's main strategy is to distract and to discourage. Therefore, after the Holy Spirit speaks to us, the devil inevitably will try to dislodge the word that God gave, by suggesting we look at outside information. This is so clearly brought out as we read Hebrews 11.

*'These all died in faith, not having received the promises, but having seen them afar off were assured of them, embraced them and confessed that they were strangers and pilgrims on the earth. For those who say such things declare plainly that they seek a homeland. And truly **if they had called to mind** that country from which they had come out, they would have **had opportunity to return.'***

(Hebrews 11:13–15)

The temptation when we have heard inside information from God, is to look back at outside information dictated by circumstances. Usually there is a time of 'insecurity' when we question God's faithfulness and ability to bring His word to pass. But how pleased God is when we choose to believe the inside information.

> *'But now they desire a better, that is, a heavenly country. Therefore **God is not ashamed to be called their God**, for He has prepared a city for them.'*   (Hebrews 11:16)

It is well!

There was a woman from Shunem who, no doubt, had given up all hope of ever having a child of her own. However, her selflessness and willingness to provide a place for the prophet to stay was not overlooked by God.

> *'And she said to her husband, "Look now, I know that this is a holy man of God, who passes by us regularly. Please, let **us** make a small upper room on the wall; and let us put a bed for him there, and a table and a chair and a lampstand; so it will be, whenever he comes to us, he can turn in there."'*
> (2 Kings 4:9–10)

God certainly honored her.

> *'And it happened one day that he came there, and he turned into the upper room and lay down there. Then he said to Gehazi his servant, "Call this Shunammite woman." When he had called her, she stood before him. And he said to him, "Say now to her, '**Look, you have been concerned for us with all this care. What can I do for you?**'"'*
> (2 Kings 4:12–13)

When she indicated she had no need, Elisha's servant told him,

> *'Actually, she has no son, and her husband is old.'*
> (2 Kings 4:14)

The prophet proclaimed to her the word of the Lord,

> *'Then he said, "**About this time next year you shall***
> *embrace a son." And she said, "No, my lord, Man of God,*
> *do not lie to your maidservant!"'* (2 Kings 4:16)

The news must have overwhelmed her, seeming too good to be true. But it was true!

> *'But the woman conceived, and bore a son when the*
> *appointed time had come, of which Elisha had told her.'*
> (2 Kings 4:17)

One can only imagine her joy and fulfillment and praise to God for having a child of her own after she had lived many years with no hope of ever having a child. How much she must have cherished and enjoyed every moment with the child – her own flesh and blood. This gift of God, unquestionably beyond her wildest dreams, must have brought indescribable fulfillment and gratification into her life.

But she was severely tested. This precious boy – this fulfilled promise from God – died.

> *'And the child grew. Now it happened one day that he went*
> *out to his father, and to the reapers. And he said to his*
> *father, "My head, my head!" So he said to a servant, "Carry*
> *him to his mother." When he had taken him and brought*
> *him to his mother, he sat on her knees until noon, **and then***
> *****died.'*** (2 Kings 4:18–20)

This fine believing woman, now shaken to the core of her being, had to choose to live by **inside information**, or lose her child of promise. She chose audaciously to 'look' into the realm of the Spirit. The first thing she did was lay the boy upon the bed of the man of God. Then she made immediate plans to go the man of God.

> *'Then she called to her husband, and said, "Please send me*
> *one of the young men and one of the donkeys, that I may run*
> *to the man of God and come back." So he said, "Why are you*

going to him today? It is neither the New Moon nor the Sabbath." And she said, "It is well."'   (2 Kings 4:22–23)

How tempting it must have been for this precious woman to capitulate to the 'reality' of the situation, and make plans to bury her son. **Outside information** certainly declared that she should face the facts and just hang on to the good memories of him. But thank God, she didn't give in! She didn't offer an explanation to her husband. She didn't get into a dialogue of unbelief with him, but instead made haste to approach the man of God. She only offered to him the authenticity of what was going on in her spirit, 'It is well!' She knew God didn't lie, neither did He change His mind. This child that came only as a result of His word, would indeed live.

Again she had to declare **inside information**.

'And so she departed, and went to the man of God at Mount Carmel. So it was, when the man of God saw her afar off, that he said to his servant Gehazi, "Look, the Shunammite woman! Please run now to meet her, and say to her, 'Is it well with you? Is it well with your husband? Is it well with the child?' " And she answered, "It is well."'

(2 Kings 4:25–26)

She refused to concede and reveal her problem to the servant of the prophet, but merely spoke the **reality** in her heart – 'It is well.' When she finally reached the man of God, and said,

'Did I ask a son of the Lord? Did I not say, "Do not deceive me?"'   (2 Kings 4:28)

She returned to the source, the original promise of God. She knew the word of the Lord had come from the mouth of the prophet, and therefore she had to resist the temptation of dialoging with anyone along the way. In essence, she was saying, 'I know you're a prophet, and why would you deliver me the promise of God and then take it away?' She was tenacious in her persistence.

> *'And the mother of the child said, "As the Lord lives, and as your soul lives, I will not leave you."'* (2 Kings 4:30)

The Shunammite woman was the perfect example of living by inside information. She clung to the promise of God, and refused to believe the report that the promise was aborted. Her son was a direct result of God speaking into her life, so she rightfully 'held' God to His word. How many times has the enemy tried to abort or kill our vision that we know came from God?

It is such a temptation when we are facing a hard place to look outwardly and to the opinions of others. Well meaning people say things such as 'I had a friend who died from the very same thing.'

The prophet, Elisha, returned to her house.

> *'When Elisha came into the house, there was the child, lying dead on his bed. He went in therefore, shut the door behind the two of them, and prayed to the Lord. And he went up and lay on the child, and put his mouth on his mouth, his eyes on his eyes, and he stretched himself out on the child, and the flesh of the child became warm. He returned and walked back and forth in the house, and again went up and stretched himself out on him; then the child sneezed seven times, and the child opened his eyes. And he called Gehazi and said, "Call this Shunammite woman." So he called her. And when she came into him, he said, "Pick up your son." So she went in, fell at his feet, and bowed to the ground, then she picked up her son and went out.'* (2 Kings 4:32–37)

Let us cross over to the other side

Jesus told His disciples, *'Let us cross over to the other side'* (Mark 4:35). When Jesus gave this declaration, clearly the disciples expected they were going to do just that. But they hadn't sailed far when a great windstorm arose. *'... and the waves beat into the boat, so that it was already filling.'* The disciples, in a desperate and frantic state, found Jesus in the stern, asleep on a pillow. Waking Him they said, *'Teacher, do you not care that we are perishing?'*

Inside information from the mouth of Jesus had already declared they were indeed going to the other side. But circumstances didn't coincide with His declaration. So often when God speaks into our lives, things immediately begin to seem the opposite. All kinds of storms and bedlam break loose. Sometimes it is simply the devil's attempt to dislodge the word that God has given to us.

While ministering in Texas, the Holy Spirit spoke one evening that a young woman was present who suffered with migraine headaches. I asked whoever was suffering this way to acknowledge it. A pleasant twenty-seven-year-old woman acknowledged it was she. We all prayed with her for a moment, **agreeing** with the oracle of the Lord concerning her. She told us that she had suffered with migraine headaches every single day of her life for as long as she could remember. I couldn't wait to see her the following evening to ask her how she felt. 'Today, I've had the worst migraine I've ever had in my life,' she told me. But that didn't bother me, because I recognized how the enemy tries hard to thwart and dislodge what God says. I encouraged her, reminding her that God doesn't lie. When I approached her the following night, she had a big grin on her face. 'Today is the first day of my life that I can remember not having a headache,' she exclaimed. And her headaches never returned.

In the middle of this storm, Jesus got up and rebuked it.

> *'Then He arose and rebuked the wind, and said to the sea, "Peace, be still! And the wind ceased and there was a great calm."* (Mark 4:39)

Then He rebuked the disciples!

> *'He said to them, "Why are you so fearful? How is it that **you** have no faith?"'* (Mark 4:40)

It seems obvious that the storm was demonic in origin,

because Jesus had to rebuke it. He upbraided them for not rebuking it, indicating that they indeed had authority over their circumstance. But it becomes even more clear that the storm was demonic because of the destination of Jesus and the disciples. What awaited them on the other side was a tremendously needy man whom Jesus was commissioned to deliver. No wonder the enemy tried to stop the boat. But Jesus meant what He said, *'Let us go to the other side.'*

Go your way, your son lives

A desperate nobleman was put on the spot to act on the words of Jesus. His son was very sick, and hearing about Jesus, he came to make his plea.

> *'When he heard that Jesus had come out of Judea into Galilee, he went to Him and implored Him to come down and heal his son, for he was at the point of death.'*
> (John 4:47)

But Jesus didn't go to pray for the man's son. Instead, He used the instance to challenge the man and all who were listening.

> *'Unless you people see signs and wonders, you will by no means believe.'* (John 4:48)

Up to this point, the miracles that Jesus performed on people were by the laying on of hands. That was all that people could understand – they would not believe unless they saw Jesus touch the person. But this situation was different! Jesus wanted to take the people to a higher level – of believing the **spoken word**. Instead of going to the nobleman's house and praying for his dying son, He sent him away! But as He sent him away, He gave him 'inside information' which was His word of promise.

> *'The nobleman said to Him, "Sir, come down before my child dies!" Jesus said to Him, "Go your way; your son lives."'*
> (John 4:49–50)

You can almost hear the desperation in the nobleman's 'tone', believing this was the final and only chance for his son to live. How excruciating it must have been for him. No doubt he had heard of Jesus personally touching people and healing them. But Jesus declared He was not physically going to his house – rather He encouraged him to believe the creative word. Imagine the struggle he must have had! The thought must have gone through his mind, 'What if I get home and my son is dead?' But the nobleman **chose to believe** the inside information that the Lord gave.

> *'So the **man believed the word that Jesus spoke to him**, and he went his way.'*   (John 4:50)

The Holy Spirit frequently gives us inside information when we are in a crisis. We must make a decision to choose to believe what He says. He will never disappoint.

> *'And as he was going down, his servants met him and told him, saying, "**Your son lives!**" Then he inquired of them the hour when he got better. And they said to him, "Yesterday at the seventh hour the fever left him." So the father knew that it was at the same hour in which Jesus said to him, "Your son lives." And he himself believed, and his whole household.'*   (John 4:51–53)

Chapter 4

Don't Abort the
Creative Word of God

- Anything God says is filled with creative power, and whatever He says ... already exists.

While preaching in a young, growing church in Kentucky, I was so mindful of the Lord's presence in an unusually intense way. The Holy Spirit began to speak concerning personal needs of those present, and we were all in awe of the way He was moving and addressing situations. At one point, a word came that God was healing someone in his bowels. I assumed it pertained to an older person, who may be having a struggle in that area of his body. But before I could give a word of explanation, a small girl raised her hand high in the air. Thinking momentarily that she misunderstood, I almost ignored her, which would have aborted what the Holy Spirit was desiring to do. But as I glanced at her parents, they were nodding their heads knowingly. So I prayed briefly with her as those present graciously came in agreement with the prayer.

Later, the couple told me their daughter, Leah, was only seven years old, but had battled a bowel problem since birth. For the first seven years of her life, she would go for extended periods without being able to have a bowel movement. Many trips to the doctor, a fourth a cup of Milk of Magnesia daily, enemas and suppositories hadn't helped. Her condition was diagnosed as Chronic Functional Constipation. At least once a week, over those first seven years of her life, her parents had to let her have a bowel movement in a bathtub full of warm water, as that was the only way her body would function.

However, even then her body would tear and bleed. When they took her to the children's hospital, the best explanation the doctors could give was that her body had an unusual reaction time. Specifically, that her bowels would be backed up for days before letting her system know. The mother told me that even after the discouraging tests, the Lord had assured her that it was going to be okay. Medical science was not able to help her, but since that evening over two years ago when the creative word was embraced, she has not had another problem!

It troubled me how close I came to ignoring Leah, because in my (puny) mind, I assumed it was an older person who had the bowel problem.

The analytical mind – the abortionist

Peter almost aborted the creative flow of the Holy Spirit when Jesus spoke to him.

> *'When Jesus had stopped speaking, He said to Simon, "Launch out into the deep and let down your nets for a catch." **But Simon answered and said to Him, "Master, we have toiled all night and caught nothing."**'*
>
> (Luke 5:4–5)

The mind commits abortions! Peter's response was sensible. He was a fisherman and was more than familiar with the time cycles. Their brains are saying, 'Huh?' They had spent the entire night without results. It was futile. Common sense avowed it was too late and it was best to wait for another day.

This is where most of us quench the Spirit. The Lord speaks to us, but the mind takes over and reasons away the thought or command God gave us. We abort the work of the Spirit by **dismissing** the thoughts of God.

In this situation, Peter caught himself, and prevented the abortion that he nearly caused by his reasoning mind. Thank God for his reaction, *'**Nevertheless at Your word I will let down the net.**'* Peter had been around Jesus enough to acknowledge, 'Nevertheless.'

So overwhelming were the results as the net filled with

fish, that Peter saw his own humanity and helplessness, saying *'Depart from me, I'm a sinful man.'*

But Jesus didn't agree with him by addressing the subject of Peter's secret sin or hang-ups. He simply declared, *'Fear not, for from now on you will catch men.'*

In essence, Jesus tells Peter that if he will learn to obey God's impulses (which obviously is of utmost priority in the mind of God), the result will be far greater than catching fish, and he will bring souls into the Kingdom.

This clearly indicates that Jesus is the soul-winner, and all fruitfulness comes by listening and having an obedient response. Real fruit is not a product of strong and determined minds, but a result of listening and refusing to let the analytical mind abort the plan of God.

God doesn't need our input. When He speaks, He calls forth results that have nothing to do with the natural. The natural or carnal mind is enmity (hostility) against God (Romans 8:7). Therefore, our puny brain is an abrasive to the Holy Spirit. God is the Author of our faith and, frankly, He doesn't respect our opinion when He declares what He is going to do. He hates unbelief, specifically when the mind scrutinizes what He is calling into existence.

Lord, if it's You, command me to come

We must be careful to avoid presumption and let God initiate things in our lives. When Jesus came walking on water toward Peter and the disciples, they were afraid. Not only were they in a life-threatening storm, they were being approached by what they thought was an apparition. But Jesus comforted them by saying, *'Be of good cheer! It is I; do not be afraid'* (Matthew 14:27).

I appreciate what Peter said in his impulsiveness:

> *'Lord, if it is You, command me to come to You on the water.'*   (Matthew 14:28)

I don't want to attempt anything without His command, lest I fall in foolish presumption. But it is okay to say, 'Lord, if it is you ...'

Thank God that the burden is on His shoulders, and we can avoid moving on our own impulses.

> *'Keep back Your servant also from presumptuous sins.'*
> (Psalm 19:13)

And it was the Lord who spoke the creative word to Peter, saying, 'Come.' In a very true sense, Peter didn't walk on the water – he walked on the word! He would never have walked on the water if Jesus hadn't said, 'Come.'

Many err by presumptuously saying what God didn't say, or by doing what God didn't command. God has taken the work out of this Gospel message, because He supplies the direction and command. Our 'work' is to live with the responsibility of listening and responding to the Spirit.

The Holy Spirit broods over us

God always desires to do more in the life of the believer. He broods over us, desiring to 'impregnate' us with a strategy from heaven. However, we are often to blame for aborting His thoughts because they don't seem reasonable or convenient.

When we understand that the Holy Spirit broods over us, then we can learn to be on guard against our mind aborting the flow of the Spirit of God, and embrace what He is saying.

At creation, God brooded over the face of the waters.

> *'The earth was without form, and void; and darkness was on the face of the deep. **And the Spirit of God was hovering (brooding)** over the face of the waters.'*   (Genesis 1:2)

God broods over His people. He desires to give birth to something new in our lives. He is the Creator! Every word He speaks is creative and gives birth to life, but we have to be so careful not to abort what He is bringing forth.

Consider this day in the life of Jesus.

> *'Now it happened on a certain day, as He was teaching, that there were Pharisees and teachers of the law sitting by, who*

had come out of every town of Galilee, Judea, and Jerusalem.
And the power of the Lord was present to heal them.'
(Luke 5:17)

Although it plainly says that the power of God was present to heal these Pharisees and teachers of the law, there is no record of any one of the Pharisees or teachers being healed! Why? Because the **analytical mind of man took over.** When a paralyzed man was lowered through the roof in front of Jesus, He recognized the faith of the men and said, *'Man, your sins are forgiven you'* (Luke 5:20).

But as soon as Jesus made that statement, reasoning took over.

'And the scribes and the Pharisees **began to reason,** *saying, "Who is this who speaks blasphemies? Who can forgive sins but God alone?"'* (Luke 5:21)

Jesus confronted their reasoning hearts, giving them opportunity to repent and 'see'.

'But when Jesus perceived their thoughts, He answered and said to them, "Why are you reasoning in your hearts? Which is easier to say, 'Your sins are forgiven you,' or to say, 'Rise up and walk?' But that you may know that the Son of Man has power on earth to forgive sins" – He said to the man who was paralyzed, "I say to you, arise, take up your bed, and go to your house." Immediately he rose up before them, took up what he had been lying on, and departed to his own house, glorifying God.' (Luke 5:25)

Clearly, God had intentions to do more. His power was present to heal. But the only one healed was the paralyzed man, because the reasoning brains of those listening and watching aborted the purpose of God.

The need to surrender the brain

These two had been praying for a son for as long as they could remember. Their names were Zacharias and Elizabeth.

They were committed and righteous people, serving the Lord faithfully for years. Their reputation was impeccable and they walked blamelessly before God.

The day came when God fulfilled the answer to their prayer. The promise came while Zacharias was in the temple offering incense. The angel of the Lord, Gabriel, stood before him and gave him the following message as Zacharias shook in fear.

> *'Do not be afraid, Zacharias, for your prayer is heard: and your wife Elizabeth will bear you a son, and you shall call his name John.'*   (Luke 1:13)

The angel continued to declare the awesome destiny on the life of their son whom God was calling forth into existence, saying,

> *'Many will have joy and gladness at his birth ... he will be great in the sight of the Lord ... he will drink neither wine nor strong drink ... he will be filled with the Holy Spirit even from his mother's womb ... he will turn many of the children of Israel to the Lord their God. He will also go before Him in the spirit and power of Elijah to turn the hearts of the fathers to the children and the disobedient to the wisdom of the just, to make ready a people prepared for the Lord.'*   (Luke 1:14–17)

One would think this wonderful man of God would be excited. He saw an angel. The angel promised him the child they had prayed for years for, and described a great portion of the life he would live. But Zacharias did the unthinkable. He didn't believe it!

The angel is angry

I've never seen an angel, but if I ever do see one, I don't want to make him mad.

Zacharias heard the word of the Lord, the very promise he and his wife had been believing for. Yet when the word came, instead of rejoicing in it, he analyzed it. He not only analyzed it, but he had the audacity to give the angel 'unknown' information.

> *'How shall I know this? For I am an old man, and my wife is*
> *well advanced in years?'*   (Luke 1:18)

Gabriel's reply is filled with a strong reprimand.

> *'I am Gabriel* (not just some Joe that walked in here),
> *who stands in the presence of God* (that's my job), *and was*
> *sent to speak to you and bring you these* (read my lips) **glad**
> **tidings.'**   (Luke 1:19)

I wonder if Gabriel might have reminded him, 'You're the one who was praying for a child.'

The angel's anger had nothing to do with the devil, or some great sin (Zacharias was a righteous man), but the fact that the **mind of man** analyzed and tried to **abort** the very word of God. Gabriel immediately declares the penalty for unbelief.

> *'But behold, you will be mute and not able to speak until the*
> *day these things take place, because you did not believe*
> *my words which will be fulfilled in their own time.'*
>   (Luke 1:20)

Here is the potent truth: **If we don't yield our mind to God, we'll lose our voice for God.**

Gabriel, who spoke for God, was angry. Can there be anything more offensive to God than unbelief? It is the analytical mind that is guilty of aborting the proceeding word of God.

The Holy Spirit was brooding over Zacharias that day in the temple. Zacharias, although a wonderful and righteous man, was guilty of nearly aborting the word of God, and would have, had not God overruled his unbelief.

How frequently the Holy Spirit broods over us, desiring to birth something new and fresh in our lives. But how often our brain, acting as some self-appointed filter, sifts out the creative word with which the Holy Spirit had intended to impregnate us. This has nothing to do with the devil, but it is the proud and unyielding mind that stands in God's way.

Let it be unto me according to Your word

God's way to bring forth fruit and change in our lives is similar to the way a woman conceives in her womb and gives birth to a child.

When the same angel, Gabriel, approached the young, innocent, virgin Mary, he made a proclamation that would have blown the mind of any normal person. But God always comes to the 'virgin' – the one who doesn't profess to know everything, but has the quality of being pure and receptive. Our minds often demand detailed information, which puts us in control. But God wants to bypass the scrutinizing mind.

As Mary heard the words spoken by this huge angel, *'Do not be afraid, Mary, for you have found favor with God. And behold, you will conceive in your womb and bring forth a Son, and shall call His name Jesus...'* she didn't demand any information except to say, *'How can this be, since I do not know a man?'* This was not an analytical question of unbelief, but rather a question of morality ... 'I'm not married.'

Gabriel has no problem with that question, *'The power of the Highest will overshadow you.'* In other words, 'Don't worry, the Holy Spirit will brood over you and cause you to conceive.'

This is the way Jesus is birthed in every Christian. Becoming a Christian is not learning a set of beliefs. It is a divine overshadowing by the Holy Spirit, combined with our willingness to say 'Be it unto me.' This is not a mental assent or exercise, but a conception, namely the person of Christ being birthed in our hearts. This is also the way He brings forth the vision He has called us to, as well as specific manifestations, events and purposes in our lives. They are birthed.

The prophet is angry

Here is another situation where the mind attempts to abort

the purpose of God. There couldn't have been a greater crisis. The famine was so severe that two women argued over eating their sons in order to survive. When the king of Israel heard the argument the two women were having, he tore his clothes. It is hard to imagine their desperation. One woman explains,

> 'This woman said to me, "Give me your son that we may eat him today, and we will eat my son tomorrow." So we boiled my son and ate him. And I said to her on the next day, "Give me your son that we may eat him"; but she has hidden her son.' (2 Kings 6:28–29)

In the middle of this horrible dilemma, the Word of the Lord comes through the prophet, Elisha.

> 'Tomorrow about this time a seah of fine flour shall be sold for a shekel, and two seahs of barley for a shekel, at the gate of Samaria.' (2 Kings 7:1)

This is awesome mind-boggling news – that in one day things would drastically change. But notice how the assistant to the king responds.

> 'So an officer on whose hand the king leaned answered the man of God and said, "**Look, if the Lord would make windows in heaven, could this thing be?**"' (2 Kings 7:2)

Elisha's rebuttal is brief and blunt.

> 'In fact, you shall see it with your eyes, but you shall not eat of it.' (2 Kings 7:2)

God will always perform His word, but His word can be aborted (where it would have been to our benefit) by **our response**. Just as Gabriel was angry with the response of Zacharias, Elisha was angry with the response of this aid to the king, and pronounced on him the declaration that he would see it but not partake of it. Of course the man died.

> *'Now the king had appointed the officer on whose hand he leaned to have charge of the gate. But the people trampled him in the gate, **and he died, just as the man of God had said, who spoke when the king came down to him.***'*
>
> (2 Kings 7:17)

The devil opposes the creative

There is nothing the enemy opposes more than the creative word of God to His people. The devil takes the opportunity of our analytical minds to encourage us to reject anything that we can't logically filter through our tiny brain. If we want God to make us fruitful, we must let Him impregnate us with His initiative and declare as Mary did, *'Be it unto me, according to **Your** word.'*

The enemy uses distractions, discouragement and countless other tools, capitalizing on the carnal and resistant mind to cause an abortion of what God is brooding over us to birth forth.

Every vision God gives to His people must first be birthed, just as a baby must be conceived in the womb of a mother. If the Bible is true, then real fruit must be the result of the birthing of His initiative, not ours. Jesus said,

> *'The words that I speak to you I do not speak on My own authority* (initiative)*; but the Father who dwells in Me does the works.'*   (John 14:10)

Many 'ministries' have never been birthed by the Holy Spirit, but are merely an act of man planning to do something for God, rather than a vision birthed in the purpose of God. Only that which God calls forth and gives life to is recognized in His sight.

Mary couldn't have declared herself to be the mother of God. Paul couldn't have declared himself a missionary to the Gentiles.

Man shall not live by bread alone...

God's design for the church is that we live and operate by the initiatives of God that daily come from His mouth. He literally has taken on all the responsibility of bringing results in our lives, but sometimes it takes us much of our lifespan to grasp this understanding.

> *'And you shall remember that the Lord your God led you all the way these forty years in the wilderness, to humble you and test you, to know what was in your heart, whether you would keep His commandments or not. So He humbled you, allowed you to hunger, and fed you with manna which you did not know nor did your fathers know,* **that He might make you know** *that man shall not live by bread alone;* **but man lives by every word that proceeds from the mouth of the Lord.'*   (Deuteronomy 8:2–3)

We all seem to be slow to learn that the **only** way to be fruitful is this truth; we have to hear the proceeding word from the mouth of God – **daily**. He allowed the Israelites to live in the wilderness, to be humbled, and to depend on Him for the manna daily – all to teach them this one truth.

This is the most exciting way to live, because God is always talking. And if we learn to pay attention, we can live in a dimension of God that is free from the typical sweat of attempting to please God by our performance. Instead we are commissioned to live by responding to His initiatives.

The problem of control

Man wants to initiate, but that is God's part. Our part is to listen and be open to the creative word. This is the most difficult thing for our human nature to grasp. Our nature wants to **earn** its way. We like to be in charge and in control. But God 'thinks'. He knows what He's doing. His design is that we listen and obey. Jesus is our example. He said,

> *'Most assuredly, I say to you, the Son can do nothing of Himself, but what He sees the Father do; for whatever He does, the Son also does in like manner.'*   (John 5:19)

Jesus did **nothing** until He either heard it or saw it from the Father. He was the perfect expression of the Father's will.

The Gospel means good news and the good news is that the burden is on God.

> *'For My yoke is easy and My burden is light.'*
> (Matthew 11:30)

The New Covenant is a listening (paying attention) Covenant.

There is overbearing control from the pulpits in many churches. Some pastors have such a fear of things getting out of control that they have a tendency to rule with too much authority. The result is the Spirit is quenched. People do not feel free to yield to the Holy Spirit because of the fear of being publicly rebuked or embarrassed. Many times there is an unwritten rule, 'We **believe** in the supernatural, but don't welcome it.'

But if the Spirit is allowed to move, He will continually amaze us.

The word creates

It is awesome that the Holy Spirit speaks to us; but consider the fact that anything He says is creative. He is calling things into existence, **if** we embrace what He is saying.

For example, one afternoon I was preparing for ministry that evening in a church in Indiana. I felt by the Spirit that I was to ask Him to give me a specific word for that church. I remember sitting on the carpeted floor of the motel room, and seeking the Lord to give me something for the congregation. As I prayed and listened, suddenly I heard the still quiet voice of the Lord say, 'There is going to be a knock at the door.' So that night when I was ministering to the people, I shared with them the message that God had given me, 'There is going to be a knock at the door.'

I wasn't aware that the church for seven years had tried to

buy land that was adjacent to their property so they could build a larger sanctuary. For the seven-year duration the landowner flatly refused to sell. However, one morning a few weeks following that meeting, the pastor and his associate were in the church office when they heard a knock at the door.

In jest, they looked at each other and said, 'This must be the knock at the door that God was talking about.' When they went to the door, it was indeed the owner of the adjacent land, declaring, 'I've decided to sell this land, if you're ready to buy.' Naturally, they jumped at the opportunity, and within a year a beautiful sanctuary was built on the property.

There is no doubt in my mind that the word of the Lord came to me that day filled with creative power. As they received the word, the land that was previously locked up, was **loosed** by the prophetic word. Although they had prayed and stood for seven years, the creative word broke the resistance and quickly brought the manifestation to pass. Because the creative word was spoken and embraced, the land was made available.

Numerous times I have witnessed the exciting fulfillment of a child granted to a couple who could not conceive. On these occasions, a word would come forth from the Holy Spirit indicating that there was a couple present that was not able to conceive. As the couple received the word, usually within less than a year there would be an announcement that they were indeed expecting. Many times, medical science has told a couple that they would not be able to have a child, but God's word goes forth with power to create what is lacking, or strengthen the weakness in their physical bodies. Often as time passes, the couple is not only blessed with the child the Lord spoke about, but additional children follow. It reminds me of Hannah who asked the Lord for one child, and the Lord spoke through Eli,

> *'Go in peace, and the God of Israel grant your petition which you have asked of Him.'*   (1 Samuel 1:17)

The Lord only spoke of one child (that is all she asked for), yet we see that the word that comes is often perpetual for she had five more children.

> *'And the Lord visited Hannah, so that she conceived and bore three sons and two daughters. Meanwhile the child Samuel grew before the Lord.'*   (1 Samuel 2:21)

The purpose of the prophetic realm

The realization that God talks to His people is awesome, and if that isn't exciting enough, everything He says has creative power! When Andrew brought Simon to Jesus, Jesus looked at Simon and spoke these words,

> *'You are Simon the son of Jonah. You shall be called Cephas.'*   (John 1:42)

The name Cephas means 'stone' or 'rock'. The 'reality' was that there was nothing rock-like about Simon. In fact, he was probably the least stable of all the disciples. But Jesus was speaking that creative word, which **calls into existence** that which does not exist. And these creative words came to pass because it was Peter who stood like a rock on the day of Penetcost, and preached a powerful sermon, where three thousand were added to the church instantly. In Peter's sermon, he pointed his long finger at the crowd, and fearless of the ramifications, declared,

> *'You have taken by lawless hands, have crucified* (Jesus of Nazareth)*, and put Him to death.'*   (Acts 2:23)

This is the same Peter who formerly stood in front of a servant girl, saying, *'Woman, I do not know Him'* (Luke 22:57).

It was an identical principle when God called Abraham to be the father of a multitude when He was still childless. God ignores the natural and calls forth the results of His creative power.

*'(As it is written, "I have made you a father of many nations") in the presence of Him whom he believed – God, who gives life to the dead and **calls those things which do not exist as though they did.**'* (Romans 4:17)

And consider Gideon, who was hiding behind the winepress. Yet the creative word of God through the Angel of the Lord, came to him saying,

'The Lord is with you, you mighty man of valor!' (Judges 6:12)

Talk about a creative word. There was nothing in Gideon's natural ability that warranted such a word. In fact, he was full of fear! But God calls that which doesn't exist into existence.

He speaks to every one of us the same way. He calls forth His ability in our lives, which has nothing to do with our qualifications.

Most of us quickly review our inadequacies and lack and dismiss the word of the Lord as 'too good to be true'. But if we'll receive the word and not abort it with our analytical minds, God will bring it to pass.

Whatever God says is creative – and already exists

When our son, David, was fifteen, he had already taken piano lessons for over ten years. He desperately wanted us to buy a better piano. When we told him we couldn't afford it, he went over our heads – to God. We agreed to pray and believe with him that God would provide a new piano. For nearly a year, we checked the want ads, and sought out sales, but nothing turned up that we could afford.

Then early one morning, my wife walked into the kitchen and said to me, 'Do you want to hear what the Lord spoke to me this morning?' I nodded. 'As I came out of sleep,' she said, 'The Lord spoke to me, "Your piano is here."' I jokingly walked into the living room and informed her that I didn't see any piano. But we both knew God well enough to recognize that it was settled – He had provided a piano.

Three days later, my son and I were going on an errand when the Holy Spirit directed our path. As we passed a music store we observed a huge sign plastered on the front of their building, 'Year-end inventory reduction sale.' We decided to go in and look. The store agreed on the spot to buy our old piano sight unseen and gave us an amazing year-end reduction price on a new one. Within two days our new piano was delivered and we could truly say, 'Our piano is here!'

Before our senses had any satisfaction, the manifestation of our piano was already a fact. God had spoken, 'Your piano is here,' yet there was absolutely no evidence to support that 'fact' in the natural. But this is how the Holy Spirit works. Anything He says – already exists.

God doesn't just reveal knowledge, He gives knowledge **filled** with the power to perform. For example, when Jesus told Simon his new name was Cephas (stone or rock), there was enough power in that word to make Peter into a mighty apostle. Not only was the word to Simon creative, but it **already existed** and was a fact in the mind of God, although it took nearly three years to come to pass.

This is exciting, because although circumstances may seem contrary, when God speaks into your situation, it is not something that is going to happen, it is **already so**, if we'll receive it.

Therefore, any time God speaks, it is not something that is **going** to be so, rather it already **is** so. Circumstances sometimes have to 'catch up' to what God has already called a fact.

In prophecy, God commits Himself to your situation

When the creative word of the Lord comes to a person directly or through another person, or by a dream, a vision, or a scripture made 'alive', it is a potent promise and commitment from the Lord to your situation. That is not to say it will happen instantly, but God is giving His personal commitment to bring fulfillment to you.

'So shall My word be that goes forth from My mouth; it shall not return to Me void, but it shall accomplish what I please. And it shall prosper in the thing for which I sent it.'

(Isaiah 55:11)

The word comes as substance or concrete for you to stand on. There are times when immediately following the word from the Lord, all circumstances appear to oppose what God said. For example, I made a return visit to a wonderful church in Pennsylvania, and a large man came up and stood in front of me. His size was somewhat intimidating and with a serious face he said, 'When you were here last year you pointed me out and told me God was going to bless my finances.' He continued, saying, 'The very next day I lost my job.' I felt for a moment like bolting out the back door. But then his face broke into a grin and he said, 'Now, I'm in business for myself and I make three times what I was making a year ago.' I then wanted prayer for my nerves!

God tells the truth

God doesn't lie. I always emphasize that simple truth when I am involved in ministering to people. The Holy Spirit is the **Spirit of Truth**. He will **never** lie or deceive you. That is why it is of utmost importance always to have an attitude and posture of **agreeing** with the Holy Spirit. Most of the time we have no clue how God will fulfill what He has promised in our lives. But our brains are too small anyway. That is why we have to command the analytical mind to be silent (for a change) and simply put our trust in the fact that the Lord can't lie and He is faithful to fulfill His word.

'For He spoke, and it was done; He commanded, and it stood fast.'

(Psalm 33:9)

A word may come to a mom and dad that God is delivering their wayward son from drugs. Does that mean that three hours later they will return home, and see their son clothed and in his right mind, sitting at the kitchen table reading the Bible? Probably not. But what God is saying is that as they receive the creative word, He is setting things in motion for the process to begin for their son's deliverance. Look out devil because God has spoken, and your hold on that young man is coming to an end. It may take weeks or months, but God is saying He is committed to them and their dilemma, and the end result is they will see their son delivered and leading a normal life free from drugs.

Recently a man approached me in the city where I was speaking. He shared with me that three years ago I was led to pray for him, and the prophetic word began to flow regarding his occupation. A portion of the word the Lord delivered to him was '...within a year, you'll be saying, "Lord, You've taken me so far."' His job situation was very weak and shortly thereafter his work load became so slight that he was phased out. But he felt strongly impressed of the Lord to start his own business. A year later, with his new business beginning to prosper, he happened to be driving past the place he had formerly worked. As he glanced over at his former employer, he said to the Lord, 'Lord, You've taken me so far.' It was then that he suddenly remembered the word of prophecy where the Holy Spirit had said that he would look back in a year and say, 'You've taken me so far.'

A high school girl was a member of a church in a small town in Iowa. When I was preaching in the church recently, she approached me and said, 'Last year you prayed for several of the youth in the church. As you prayed for me, you said that God was going to make me an excellent student.' She told me, 'I knew within myself that you had missed God and that there was no way that could pertain to me. I consistently get Ds on my report card.' Now, however, she explained with a big smile, 'I am getting nearly straight As.' She was in total amazement at the creative result of the word of the Lord. So was I.

Teeth straightened by the creative word

On a Sunday morning in a small church in Indiana, the Holy Spirit spoke that He was healing someone's child who had protruding teeth. A young mother of four jumped up, acknowledging that the dentist had recently told her and her husband that it would cost at least $5000 to have their child's teeth straightened by braces. She joyfully claimed the word and went home that afternoon, put her hand on her eight-year-old's mouth saying, 'In the name of Jesus, you are healed.' She testified later that she didn't instantly notice a change, but in less than two weeks her son's teeth were perfectly straight! His dentist was amazed and told her that the boy's teeth are the nicest of all her children. When she tells of this awesome miracle, she describes her son's former condition of his teeth by saying, 'He could eat an apple through a knothole in a fence.'

To God be the glory!

Chapter 5

Your Brain – Your Greatest Enemy

- **Worldliness** – refusing to hear the voice of God.

I was sitting across the table from a prominent California pastor who was pumping me with question after question about my experiences with the Holy Spirit. We were just becoming acquainted with one another and I was impressed with his passion for the Lord. We had been introduced by mutual friends who also were seated at the table of this restaurant. We were all engrossed in a passionate discourse and enjoying the intense presence of the Lord. Suddenly he asked me, 'Steve, why is it so important to pray in the Spirit?' Without taking a breath, I heard these words coming out of my spirit, 'Praying in tongues anesthetizes the brain.' He leaned back in his chair pondering the statement. 'I never heard that before,' he said. 'Neither had I,' I replied, recognizing that the Holy Spirit had spoken through me. I immediately turned to a doctor who was sitting at our table, and asked her, 'What is the purpose of an anesthetic?' She answered, 'An anesthetic inhibits conduction.'

We were all in awe over this truth in which the Holy Spirit had just enlightened us. The prayer language helps to 'numb' the active brain, which so often has the common reputation of interfering with the Holy Spirit. Our brain has to be 'bypassed' by the Spirit of God, so the Holy Spirit helps us by rendering it inactive (inhibiting conduction) momentarily.

The brain is a gift from God; yet it is the brain that so often aborts the voice of the Holy Spirit. In fact, so much emphasis by Christians is placed on the devil being our greatest enemy.

This is true, but the devil is a **defeated** foe. The brain, in its propensity to question the voice of the Holy Spirit, must be 'defeated' in each of our lives.

> *'Because the carnal mind is enmity* (hostility) *against God; for it is not subject to the law of God, nor indeed can be.'*
> (Romans 8:7)

The word, carnal, comes from the Greek word, *sarx*, meaning 'meat'. The 'meat mind', or 'meat head' is contrary to the mind of God. We must choose **His** mind.

Elijah put his head down

When Elijah was told by the Lord that He was going to send rain on the earth (1 Kings 18:1), Elijah still had to come into agreement and pray it forth. He went to the top of Mount Carmel and began to pray. The way he positioned himself in prayer was significant.

> *'And Elijah went up to the top of Carmel;* **then he bowed down on the ground, and put his face between his knees.'** (1 Kings 18:42)

Putting his face between his knees represents not only humility, but the need to submit the brain to the Spirit of God. When we begin to seek God, it is such a temptation to let the mind wander, analyze and question how (and if) God is going to answer.

It is noteworthy that Elijah stayed stationary with his head still down, while telling his servant to *'Go up now, look toward the sea'* (1 Kings 18:43). The servant represents **faith**! We have to tell our faith to 'go check' and see what is happening. Going to check is an act of expectation – you are expecting results!

The servant went seven times before seeing any results. Every time the servant came back saying, 'There is nothing.' Elijah just told him, 'Go again.' This represents not only expectation, but a divine stubbornness – convinced that God is going to answer.

Although the answer seemed slow in coming, every time the servant ran to check, his anticipation must have been stretched. When we activate our faith and begin to check – knowing God is answering, it is always a faith-stretching experience.

When the servant finally came back with the report that he saw a cloud the size of a man's hand, it didn't sound like much. But when God begins to move, the ramifications will be mighty.

I encourage people always to have their servant (faith) to be observant and continue to check what God is doing. Especially in meetings while the anointing is present, God will bring forth healings as we anticipate Him.

When we are asking God for something, we need to stretch our faith continually and behold what He is doing. So many answers to prayer go unnoticed because we cease to remain alert and aware that God is always moving.

A good way to live is to stay in awe of God continually.

> *'By awesome deeds in righteousness You will answer us.'*
> (Psalm 65:5)

How much is this going to cost?

Jesus emphasized so graphically how the mind has to be subdued by His answer to the scribe who said, *'Teacher, I will follow You wherever You go'* (Matthew 8:19).

It is noteworthy that most of us would expect Jesus to affirm him and encourage this scribe's commitment in some way. But Jesus responded to his declaration in a surprising way.

> *'Foxes have holes, and the birds of the air have nests, but the Son of Man has nowhere to **lay His head**.'* (Matthew 8:20)

Why does Jesus answer this scribe with such a statement? He was letting the man (and us) know that choosing to follow Him means losing our head! Since we Christians are the **body** of Christ, then He is looking for a place to lay His **head**. He is saying that if we really want to follow Him fully, it is going to cost us our heads. Where He wants to lay His head – is on us! Therefore, He was letting us know that there is an ultimate **price** to pay. The price being that we no longer have the luxury of relying on our own wisdom and our own brains for guidance. We have to let Him replace our head with His – our thoughts with His thoughts. Daily, we have to desire and yield to the mind of Christ. We must be willing to pay the price to yield up our analytical and reasoning mind, and follow Him in thinking His thoughts and seeking His mind on **every** decision.

It is not enough to be saved, or to know we have had awesome experiences with the Holy Spirit. There must be a willingness and a yieldedness and desire to continually know the mind of God. No longer do we have the luxury of depending on our senses and logic, but we must seek Him.

In many conversations with Christians, it becomes apparent there is no room made for the mind of the Spirit. 'This is what I think.' 'What do you think?' These are familiar statements we all use. But the bottom line is, what does God think? We cannot find a better example to live by than Jesus. Yet Jesus said,

> *'Most assuredly, I say to you, the Son can do nothing of Himself, but what He sees the Father do; for whatever He does, the Son also does in like manner.'* (John 5:19)

And,

> *'I can of Myself do nothing. As I hear, I judge; and My judgment is righteous, because I do not seek My own will but the will of the Father who sent Me.'* (John 5:30)

We all love the new Christian slogan, WWJD (What would Jesus do?) and many even wear it in jewelry form, but do we really believe we can access God in **all** things? Yes! He will graciously grant us the directives we need.

God's enemy – your opinion

I was preparing for a trip to Illinois, where I was going to teach for a week at a training school for missionaries. Two days before departing, I thought I would pray for the school and ask God to bless the week. As I lay on the floor praying, the Holy Spirit spoke in distinct clear words, 'Their building is coming.'

The sentence was so clear that I knew it was the voice of the Lord. When I got up to speak at the first session, I repeated what the Holy Spirit said. The leader began to weep uncontrollably. I knew the Lord was confirming His word to her.

Later, she related to me, how following the word, she and the staff began to search the town for a suitable building. 'Surely,' they thought, 'God obviously has a building for us near by.' But the more they searched, the more frustrated they became. They found nothing to rent, to buy, not even land to build upon.

But God had spoken. When He speaks, things are set into motion – His words always carry creative power. After weeks of their exhaustive search for the building, an acquaintance approached the leader one day, carrying a real estate magazine. 'I was in a grocery store in a town nearby, and felt a desire to pick up this free real estate magazine. It shows this building for sale. You might want to check it out,' she said. She picked up the magazine and observed what the woman was referring to. It was a monastery for sale. It was located in a town fifty-five miles away. It was built in the shape of a huge E, and had twenty-five individual rooms with private bathrooms, a chapel, a library and a kitchen. She and the board members drove over to look at it. It was in pristine, flawless condition, although it was over two decades old. 'Could it be possible' they pondered, 'to actually move the building to their property?'

That is when I received the call from them.

'Do you remember the word you had for us about our building coming?' she asked. I affirmed that I did. She began to tell me about this building they had found, and told me several details regarding it, talking for several minutes. 'Would you mind asking the Lord about it and calling us back in thirty minutes?' she asked.

As soon as we hung up, I went into my living room and sat on my recliner and began to pray. Immediately, however, although I tried earnestly to pray, I felt my mind scanning the details she had related to me about the building. The more my mind scrutinized the facts I had absorbed, the more I thought this cannot be the building that God has for them.

Suddenly I heard the voice of the Lord in my spirit. '**The worse thing you can give anyone . . .**' He said, '**is your opinion.**' I'll never forget the words. I stood rebuked. God knew I was on the verge of offering the conclusion of my puny brain, instead of His will and thoughts on the matter. Gladly, I called her back, and told her my experience. Obviously, the Lord was clearly indicating to go ahead with it.

Within weeks, a contractor was hired, who for a modest price, cut the building in sixteen sections and hauled it piece by piece the fifty-five mile trip to their town. Contractors on the other end had already poured concrete footings to match the exact size of the building segments.

The day the first piece of the building was en route, they stood at the edge of the interstate joyfully saying, 'Here comes our building!' They of course were recalling the original word of the Lord months previous, 'Your building is coming.'

The last enemy to be defeated

We spend so much time blaming the devil, but the real cause of many of our problems is no more than our brain. The analytical mind can be the greatest hindrance to the Holy Spirit, because the natural mind is an enemy (a hostile enemy) to the Spirit of God.

> '*Because the carnal* (natural) *mind is enmity against God; for it is not subject to the law of God, nor indeed can be.*'
> (Romans 8:7)

In order that the body of Christ can enter into total victory, the ultimate price must be paid. We must **yield** our minds to Him. Jesus was crucified at Golgotha, which means the Place of the Skull (John 19:17). This is where we must ultimately be crucified ... at the place of the skull. The brain has to be submitted and totally surrendered to the Holy Spirit.

God is willing to do more

We need to realize that the Holy Spirit is willing to do much more than we allow Him. In fact, I know as believers (unbelieving believers) we frustrate and disappoint Him, because His purpose is always to manifest Himself in a greater way. The bottom line is that God wants to move, but we must make room for Him and let Him!

Chapter 6

Gathering Fragments

- If God never did another thing for you, you couldn't live long enough to praise Him adequately for what He's already done.

'Gather up the fragments that remain, so that nothing is lost.' (John 6:12)

One of the greatest hurts we experienced in our ministry happened a few years ago when my wife felt so strongly impelled by the Lord to deliver a word of prophecy to a certain pastor. She felt the Lord had given her a prophetic word for this pastor and his wife that God was going to bless them with a child, and she was confident that the Holy Spirit showed her it would be a girl. My wife had no prior knowledge that this couple had been married for many years and had never been able to have children. After much prayer over several weeks, and my wife, in fear and trepidation, she finally yielded to the Lord's prompting and called the pastor at his church. She gave him the word, 'God is going to bless you and your wife with a baby, and it is going to be a girl.' There was silence on the other end, but then he quietly thanked her and the conversation ended. As often happens when we obey the Lord, my wife questioned herself, wondering if she had really heard the Lord or had made a fool of herself. It was definitely one of the most difficult words she had ever delivered.

Months passed and then we heard the news that the pastor's wife was pregnant. Of course, they, as well as family and church members, were extremely happy. Finally the day came and his wife gave birth to a baby girl. What hurt most was that we never received a phone call during this entire time. Of course this was slightly comprehensible, as we often wondered if these pastors even remotely embraced the word of the Lord unless it was through certain people. What seemed totally unacceptable, however, was when friends of ours, who also were close to the pastor, questioned him about it and he abruptly told them he remembered nothing of receiving a word of prophecy regarding a baby. It seems it would be difficult to forget such a word.

Through this experience, we began to understand how God must feel. God goes out of His way to bless us and to provide our needs. Yet how often we callously forget how He has intervened in our lives. His heart must be grieved at our lack of gratitude, and by our being remiss in not at least acknowledging the answered prayer and giving Him the glory. Just as we felt hurt by this lack of acknowledgment (not that we deserved or were looking for credit) so must He.

My wife had spent a great deal of sacrificial time praying about relaying this prophetic word. She also had to overcome the fear in her own flesh in order to make the phone call. I unequivocally believe there would not even be a baby if my wife had not listened to God and yielded to the creative word. When God gives forth a word of prophecy, it is filled with creative power. Therefore, if she had withheld the word, there is certainly a possibility that this may never have come to pass.

We have a responsibility to gather fragments

Jesus fed a huge multitude of hungry people – then made a most unusual statement,

> *'Gather up the fragments that remain, so that nothing is lost.'*   (John 6:12)

Why would He make such a statement? After all, He miraculously multiplied a boy's lunch of five barley loaves and two fish into enough quantity to feed five thousand men, not including the women and children.

> *'And Jesus took the loaves, and when He had given thanks He distributed them to the disciples, and the disciples to those sitting down; and likewise of the fish,* **as much as they wanted.***'* (John 6:11)

When everyone was filled, He concluded this awesome miracle by commanding His disciples to gather up all the remaining fragments that nothing would be lost.

It perplexed me every time I read this. Why would He give such a command to pick up all the fragments? I want to say to Him, 'You're the Son of God, just multiply more food if you want more.'

As I prayed about this, the Holy Spirit indicated to me that fragments represent **evidence** of the awesome miracle that He performed. In fact, we are always to gather 'fragments' and carry this evidence of glorious things God has performed in our lives. Christians should be a consistent walking, talking, testimony of God's goodness and faithfulness with our fragments 'in hand' as proof.

The mistake people make is that we quickly forget when God answers our prayers and provides for us, and flippantly go our way. But Jesus emphasized, *'Gather up the fragments that remain,* **so that nothing is lost.***'* We must not dare to forget the very specifics where He moved in our lives.

Poor memory

One consistent characteristic of the people of God, that goes all the way back to ancient Israel, is that of a seemingly poor memory.

> *'Nevertheless He saved them for His name's sake, that He might make His mighty power known. He rebuked the Red Sea also, and it dried up; so He led them through the depths, as through the wilderness. He saved them from the hand of him who hated them, and redeemed them from the hand of the enemy. The waters covered their enemies; there was*

*not one of them left. **Then** they believed His words; they sang His praise. **They soon forgot His works; They did not wait for His counsel.***'   (Psalm 106:8–13)

*'But He, being full of compassion, forgave their iniquity, and did not destroy them. Yes, many a time He turned His anger away, and did not stir up all His wrath; for He remembered that they were but flesh, a breath that passes away and does not come again. How often they provoked Him in the wilderness, and grieved Him in the desert! Yes, again and again they tempted God, and **limited** the Holy One of Israel. **They did not remember His power; the day when He redeemed them from the enemy.***'   (Psalm 78:38–42)

Most believers I know would readily agree that God has not only been merciful to them, but has answered countless prayers in their behalf. It seems that most of us could thankfully proclaim that, if the Lord never did another thing for us, we couldn't live long enough to thank Him adequately for all the many ways He has blessed us. God is good to His people.

But we so easily forget.

God remembers and keeps records

At a point soon following His miracle of feeding the multitude, the disciples' 'poor memory' is exposed. Jesus got into the boat with the disciples to depart to the other side. The disciples had forgotten to take bread and only had one loaf with them in the boat (Mark 8:13–14).

'And He charged them, saying, "Take heed, beware of the leaven of the Pharisees and the leaven of Herod."'

(Mark 8:15)

The disciples assume that He is talking about their lack of bread.

'And they reasoned among themselves, saying, "It is because we have no bread."'   (Mark 8:16)

Jesus was aware of their reasoning and rebuked them for being so hard hearted, and for **not remembering** the recent miracles He performed.

> *'Why do you reason because you have no bread? Do you not yet perceive nor understand? Is your **heart still hardened?** Having eyes, do you not see? And having ears, do you not hear? **And do you not remember?**'* (Mark 8:17–18)

Notice how meticulously Jesus has kept a record.

> *' "When I broke the five loaves for the five thousand, how many baskets **full of fragments** did you take up?" They said to Him, "Twelve." "Also, when I broke the seven for the four thousand, how many **large baskets full of fragments** did you take up?" And they said, "Seven." So He said to them, "How is it you do not understand?" '*
>
> (Mark 8:19–21)

God keeps records. With specific detail Jesus reminded the disciples of the magnitude of the miracle. This is a strong indication that God doesn't take lightly the miracles and answered prayers He has performed in our lives. And neither should we.

Why gather fragments?

As a pastor for a number of years, I saw first hand the need to gather fragments. One Sunday evening a woman visited our church. The Holy Spirit revealed that night, by the word of knowledge, that someone was present with a condition of breast cancer. This woman acknowledged it was she, and we prayed with her, embracing and receiving God's word to her. The power of God was revealed, as her subsequent test showed that she was totally free of cancer. We were delirious with joy for what God had done. Yet word came back to us weeks later when this same woman explained to a friend that she would never come back to our church. Unbelievably, her main excuse was she had seen a woman wearing slacks that awesome night God sovereignly healed her, and being of a strict Pentecostal background, she was offended by that. I wanted to defend our church (and God). If God wasn't offended by our church, and came and manifested Himself in such a way as to heal her of breast cancer, then who was she to say, 'I am offended?' Where were her fragments?

My wife and I also had an experience where we had counseled a woman with marriage problems over a long period of time. We spent countless sacrificial hours away from our home and children to counsel her in person, and also invested volumes of precious time on the phone with her, 'walking' her through the healing process until her marriage was completely healed. She and her husband were restored and ecstatically happy. However, one day she called us to say that she would never come back to our church because every time she attended, it reminded her of the former state of her marriage. Again I wanted to defend our ministry and God by asking her where her sense of gratitude was. And loyalty? Why didn't she have the courtesy to 'gather fragments' and be grateful for a church and ministry that helped her through such a hard time?

I wonder what the heart of God feels when we so readily forget His miracles and multiple answered prayers. What about prayers He answered that we didn't even pray? From how many things has He spared us because He chose to intervene in our lives? We should forever remain in a posture of gratitude and thanksgiving for the 'known' and 'unknown' fragments He has graciously bestowed upon each of us. His mercy is unfathomable.

In the Old Covenant there was an ignorance offering for sin:

> *'Speak unto the children of Israel, saying, If a soul shall sin through ignorance against any of the commandments of the Lord concerning things which ought not to be done, and shall do against any of them ... let him offer to the Lord for his sin which he has sinned a young bull without blemish as a sin offering.'* (Leviticus 4:2–3 KJV)

It is good for us to personally offer an 'ignorance thanksgiving offering' of thanksgiving to the Lord, daily – for things He did for us that we are unaware.

Jehoshaphat's memory

When three armies came against Jehoshaphat, he immediately began to seek the Lord.

> *'And Jehoshaphat feared, and set himself to seek the Lord, and proclaimed a fast throughout all Judah. So Judah gathered together to ask help from the Lord; and from all the cities of Judah they came to seek the Lord.'*
>
> (2 Chronicles 20:3–4)

The way Jehoshaphat prayed when he was faced with such a monumental crisis, was in stirring up the **memory** of what God had done in the past. As the people stood in agreement, this is how he prayed.

> *'O Lord God of our fathers, are You not God in heaven, and do You not rule over all the kingdoms of the nations, and in Your hand is there not power and might, so that no one is able to withstand You? Are You not our God, who drove out the inhabitants of this land before Your people Israel, and gave it to the descendants of Abraham Your friend forever? And they dwell in it, and have built You a sanctuary in it for Your name, saying, "If disaster comes upon us – sword, judgment, pestilence, or famine – we will stand before this temple and in Your presence (for Your name is in this temple), and cry out to You in our affliction, and You will hear and save."'*
>
> (2 Chronicles 20:6–9)

The key to his faith and victory was **remembering** the faithfulness of God and the deliverances He had wrought for him in the past.

We are so quick to forget the multitude of answered prayers, and the deliverances God has done for us, that we panic when a crisis comes. But we need to stir up our memory, and bring to remembrance His sovereignty bestowed on each of us. It's time to dust off our basket and bring out our fragments.

Eat at one restaurant, pay at another?

As pastors, my wife and I felt strongly led of the Spirit to minister to anyone who came through the door. We encouraged an atmosphere of freedom in the Spirit, and the word spread around our city. Therefore, it frequently happened when people had a serious need, they would come to our church, seeking a specific word of encouragement or direction, or healing from God.

Countless times the Lord would graciously meet needs, speaking to them through the gift of prophecy, and manifesting healings and miracles.

One thing, however, that frequently troubled us was the rarity of people who ever expressed any appreciation. In fact, as soon as their life was straightened out, they would go back to the large, predictably respectable church down the street where all their friends attended. That is where they would give all their tithes and offerings. Yet it was often in our midst where the Lord graciously blessed them and met their needs.

I thought to myself many times how strange it would be to eat a meal at one restaurant, then walk across the street to pay at another restaurant.

Don't carry burdens, carry baskets of fragments

I grew up with a mindset that the more miserable and burdened Christians appeared to be, the more spiritual they were, because they were carrying a cross for Christ. But now I realize that He is our burden-bearer, if we walk with Him.

> *'Take my yoke upon you and learn from Me, for I am gentle and lowly in heart, and you will find rest for your souls. **For My yoke is easy and My burden is light.**'*
>
> (Matthew 11:29–30)

The good news of the gospel is that He is in control. It is not about us; it is about Him! He is the center of our lives and His anointing (Christ is the anointed One) destroys every yoke of bondage. Notice this awesome verse about the anointing.

> *'It shall come to pass in that day that his* (the devil or the oppressor's) *burden will be taken away from your shoulder, and his yoke from your neck, and the yoke will be destroyed because of the anointing oil.'*   (Isaiah 10:27)

The burden has been taken away from our shoulders! The devil's yoke is gone. Our shoulders are not to be burdened. Instead our shoulders are to be 'carrying' the glory of God! The priests who bore the ark of God carried it on their shoulders. The presence of the Lord has replaced the burdens!

We are not to carry burdens on our shoulders, but we **are** to carry baskets! Every one of us should have an imaginary basket slung over his shoulder, filled with all the answered prayers, deliverances, and all the benefits God has given us. Then with this 'basket' present on our shoulders, each person who crosses our path will be the beneficiary of receiving a fragment from us.

David said,

> *'Bless the Lord, O my soul, **and forget not all His benefits:** Who forgives all your iniquities, Who heals all your diseases, Who redeems your life from destruction, Who crowns you with lovingkindness and tender mercies, Who satisfies your mouth with good things, so that your youth is renewed like the eagle's.'*   (Psalm 103:2–5)

Lack of gratitude

There is nothing more detestable than a lack of gratitude. When children complain and whine it has a way of penetrating the spinal chord in an almost painful state. The Bible predicted in the last days, unthankfulness would become rampant.

> *'For men will be lovers of themselves, lovers of money, boasters, proud, blasphemers, disobedient to parents, **unthankful**, unholy ... '*   (2 Timothy 3:1)

One characteristic of man, falling into perversion and degradation, was ingratitude.

> *'Because although they knew God, they did not glorify Him as God, **nor were thankful**, but became futile in their thoughts, and their foolish hearts were darkened.'*
>
> (Romans 1:21)

Ten lepers, nine poor memories

Ten lepers called out to Jesus, saying *'Jesus, Master, have mercy on us!'* (Luke 17:13).

Jesus responded to their cry and said to them, *'Go, show yourselves to the priests'* (Luke 17:14).

As they obeyed and went their way, they were healed. But only **one** of them returned to thank Jesus.

> *'And one of them, when he saw that he was healed, returned, and with a loud voice glorified God, and fell down on his face at His feet, giving Him thanks. And he was a Samaritan.'*
>
> (Luke 17:15–16)

This Samaritan sounded extremely thankful, glorifying God with a loud voice and falling down at the feet of Jesus as he gave Him thanks. It seems strange that only one man bothered to come back and thank Jesus. Yet all of them had the horrific condition of leprosy, which carries a terrible stench and decays the body of its victim.

It struck Jesus strangely as well. There is sarcasm and wonderment in His question,

> *'Were there not ten cleansed? But where are the other nine? Were there not any found who returned to give glory to God except this foreigner?'*   (Luke 17:17)

I can't comprehend how these lepers, miraculously healed, did not have the courtesy to thank Him. We all need to purpose never to be guilty of doing the same thing. It is so important to give thanks and gather the fragments of the great things He has done.

All you need is a crumb

Six years ago my wife and I did something we said we'd never do. We bought a dog who now lives in the house. I guess our children talked us into it – plus the salesperson pointed out that this animal was odorless and shedless. Anyway, we took the plunge and, in general the dog has been a blessing and a faithful companion in our household.

However, we have a standing rule concerning the dog. She eats only dog food (never human food). The veterinarian warned us not to let the dog get in the habit of eating human food. Naturally, the dog never sits at the table with us, but if you could understand dog language, she would communicate to you one truth. In so many words, the dog would say, 'I know I can't eat from your table, but anything that falls on the floor is mine.' Each meal she remains as expectant as the last that there will be new crumbs for her to enjoy.

There was a woman who came to Jesus who was a Gentile. She had a tremendous need – she desperately wanted her daughter set free of demons.

> *'For a woman whose young daughter had an unclean spirit heard about Him, and she came and fell at His feet. The woman was a Greek, a Syro-Phonecian by birth, and she **kept asking** Him to cast the demon out of her daughter.'*
> (Mark 7:25–26)

Jesus didn't grant her request, but turned her away, saying,

> *'Let the children be filled first, for it is not good to take the children's bread and throw it to the **little dogs**.'*
> (Mark 7:27)

Gentiles were often referred to as dogs, and were considered to be second-class citizens.

Rightfully, this woman should have been offended and indignant, but instead she proclaims something immensely noteworthy and phenomenal.

> *'Yes, Lord, yet even the little dogs under the table eat from
> the **children's crumbs**.'*   (Mark 7:28)

She recognized the power and ability of God! In essence
she said to Jesus, 'I don't need a smorgasbord spread before
me. I understand that there is enough power in the **crumbs**
to make my daughter well.'

What an example she is to us. We often are picky eaters,
and place demands on God to send someone to us to tell us
what God is saying, or to spoon-feed us in some manner.
But what she said to Jesus got His attention – *'Even the little
dogs under the table eat from the children's crumbs.'* She knew
that God had the ability, and all she needed was a **crumb**
to see her daughter delivered. She knew how to gather
fragments!

It is almost implied that, in effect, Jesus was letting her
know that He had no intention of granting her request; yet
He had to say, 'You got Me on that one.'

He responded to her by saying,

> *'**For this saying** go your way; the demon has gone out of
> your daughter.'*   (Mark 7:28)

He granted her request because of what **she said**. She let Him
know she understood there was enough power in the crumbs
to make her daughter well.

Looking for crumbs

I have changed my whole posture in seeking God. No longer
does it matter who is speaking at a church, or if the entire
sermon is something I must hear. Neither does it matter who
crosses my path to give me something from God. I am
looking for crumbs! God will see to it that there are always
fragments to gather up. Often, I've gleaned just one sentence
out of a sermon that was life changing.

God doesn't usually speak in long paragraphs, but often He
will speak a word or a short phrase across your spirit. If you
are attentive, that 'crumb' or 'fragment' will be just the
direction you need.

It is similar to the centurion who said to Jesus,

> *'Therefore I did not even think myself worthy to come to You. But **say the word**, and my servant will be healed.'*
>
> (Luke 7:7)

This powerful man recognized the same principle. He didn't need Jesus to spread a smorgasbord and come to his dwelling, he just needed a word – that one crumb or fragment.

> *'For I also am a man placed under authority, having soldiers under me. And I say to one, "Go," and he goes; and to another, "Come," and he comes and to my servant, "Do this," and he does it.'*
>
> (Luke 7:8)

Jesus marveled at the man's faith and understanding of this truth and said,

> *'I say to you, I have not found such **great faith**, not even in Israel.'*
>
> (Luke 7:9)

Rather than try to work up faith, we need to focus on God who will speak that one word which is a power-filled crumb. Again, we make it too difficult and complicated, demanding God speak paragraphs to us, send prophets to us, spread a huge smorgasbord, or place a flashing neon sign with specific detailed instructions in our front yard. But all we need is that one word from the sweet Holy Spirit.

Bring home the grapes!

When Moses gave the command to the twelve spies to check out the land, part of the mandate was to bring back some of the fruit of the land.

> *' "Be of good courage. **And bring some of the fruit of the land."** Now the time was the season of the first ripe grapes.'*
>
> (Numbers 13:20)

When they returned from spying out the land, they were obedient to carry home a huge cluster of grapes.

> *'Then they came to the Valley of Eshcol, and there cut down a branch with **one cluster of grapes**; they carried it between two of them on a pole. They also brought some of the pomegranates and figs.'*   (Numbers 13:23)

However, upon returning, ten of the twelve spies were consumed not with the lushness of the land, but by the **size** of the giants.

> *'Nevertheless the people who dwell in the land are strong; the cities are fortified and very large, moreover we saw the descendants of Anak there. The Amalekites dwell in the land of the South; the Hittites, the Jebusites, and the Amorites dwell in the mountains; and the Canaanites dwell by the sea and along the banks of the Jordan.'*   (Numbers 13:28–29)

God already knew they would take inventory of the giants, so He focused on gathering the grapes. Grapes make wine, and wine is representative of the joy of the Lord. His intent was that, when they saw the tremendous fruit, it would eclipse their view of the giants. In other words, if we become intoxicated with the joy of the Lord, we won't be overwhelmed with the size of the enemy. Grapes were the fragments and evidence they needed.

God's way is to let us **taste** first. David said,

> *'O taste and see that the Lord is good.'*   (Psalm 34:8)

We must willingly gather the grapes, and remember the promises of God, rather than be caught up with the lies and distortions of the enemy.

Chapter 7

Putting a Demand on
the Presence of God

We had been invited to speak at a church in New York state
that had just occupied a remodeled building. The people
were jubilant and the smell of fresh paint and sheet rock
filled the air. The pastor was excited because they had
finished off a little room in the back of the church to serve
as an evangelist's quarters. Being the first guest speakers in
the new facility, we joined in their jubilation and tried not to
complain. But the pungent odor of glue used in attaching the
paneling to the walls, combined with the freshly glued
carpet, was almost more than we could bear. We were
suffering to the point of our eyes stinging and watering
constantly, and sleep was very difficult.

The third day of our 'adventure' the phone rang. It was a
man who was active in the church and often led the worship.
He confidently proclaimed, 'I've been in prayer today, and
the Lord clearly spoke to me to bring you my credit card
and to tell you to use it to check into the Holiday Inn.' He
was firm in his statement and brought the card by within the
hour. We were overwhelmingly relieved and so very grateful
to God for His compassion toward us.

During the meeting the next night, two specific words of
knowledge the Holy Spirit spoke was that He was healing
someone with warts on his feet, and also that He was
whitening someone's teeth.

This same gentleman, who had blessed us with the hotel
room, approached me very excitedly following the service.
He told me how he felt a strong prompting from the Lord to

check his feet after the word of knowledge had come forth. With people milling around, he went over to the bench where his keyboard sat, and removed his shoes and socks. This man had been a professional roller skater for years and his feet were covered with calluses and numerous planters warts. But when he looked at his bare feet, all the warts were gone, as well as the calluses. He looked in awe as the skin on his feet had become soft and new as a baby's skin.

He beckoned for his wife to come and see the miracle which had transpired. As she stood in awe of the miracle of God giving new skin, she smiled broadly. He couldn't believe what he saw. She had always complained of her discolored teeth. But **now** her teeth were sparkling white!

I believe these two miracles were a direct result of this couple's obedience to God. They were willing to obey and provide us a more comfortable environment, and their obedience put a 'draw' on God, who mightily blessed them in return.

I've known this husband and wife for many years, and he still has flawless 'new' skin on his feet and her teeth are still white as pearls.

Living with a demand on the presence of God

One of the most misunderstood principles of faith and receiving from God is that of living with a demand on His presence.

Putting a demand on His presence is an act of faith and belief. It is living with a tenacity toward God, and recognizing His willingness to provide your need.

The mistake many people make is an attitude of 'leaving it up to God'. However, from God's perspective, He has already made provision for us. He has already set a table – a smorgasbord of enormous proportions. He will not force-feed us. We must partake on our own initiative. But He has provided all that we could possibly need, and commands us to ask.

> *'Let us therefore come **boldly** to the throne of grace, that we may obtain mercy and find grace to help in time of need.'*
>
> (Hebrews 4:16)

God touching you or you touching God?

The average person, who is even mildly hungry for God lives under the assumption that God will touch him when He is ready. But if we observe how Jesus ministered to people, that is not how it happened.

> *'And when the men of that place recognized Him, they sent out into all that surrounding region, brought to Him all who were sick, and begged Him that they might only touch the hem of His garment. And as many as touched it were made perfectly well.'*   (Matthew 14:35–36)

> *'Wherever He entered, into villages, cities, or the country, they laid the sick in the marketplaces, and begged Him that they might just touch the hem of His garment. And as many as touched Him were made well.'*   (Mark 6:56)

> *'And when she heard about Jesus, she came behind Him in the crowd and touched His garment. For she said, "If only I may touch His clothes, I shall be made well." Immediately the fountain of her blood was dried up, and she felt in her body that she was healed of the affliction.'*
> (Mark 5:27–28)

Pressing in

The provision of God, to be possessed, must be aggressively sought.

> *'For all the promises of God in Him are Yes and Amen, to the glory of God through us.'*   (2 Corinthians 1:20)

In others words, God has **already said** 'Yes' and 'Amen' concerning meeting the need that we have.

But **we** must press in for the promise. Pressing in involves asking and continuing to ask. Jesus said that we are to ask (and keep on asking), to seek (and keep on seeking), and to knock (and keep on knocking) (Luke 11:9).

Pressing in is so paramount in our walk that Jesus described it in a parable. He exhorted His disciples to pray and press in with persistence. Here the Scripture says that He taught them how to pray and not lose heart. The first thing that most experience is loss of heart – to feel that God is not interested or that God doesn't care, or that we have done something to offend Him.

Jesus likened Himself to the unrighteous judge who possessed the characteristics of having no fear of God or regard for man. This judge encountered a widow who approached him with extreme persistence that she might find justice (legal help and protection) from her adversary. The judge refused to help her at first, but then he came to a decision to help her. He said,

> *'Though I have neither reverence or fear for God nor respect or consideration for man, yet because this widow continues to* **bother** *me, I will defend and protect and avenge her; lest she give me* **intolerable annoyance and wear me out by her continual coming, or at the last she come and rail on me, or assault me, or strangle me.'**
>
> (Luke 18:4–5 AMP)

Jesus concluded the parable by exhorting us to listen to the words of the unrighteous judge. The judge had answered the woman **solely on her persistence**!

Then He said,

> *'... and will not God defend and protect and avenge His elect* (His chosen ones) *who cry to Him day and night? Will he defer them and delay help on their behalf? I tell you, He will defend and protect and avenge them speedily. However, when the Son of man comes will He find* (persistence in) *the faith on the earth?'*
>
> (Luke 18:7–8 AMP)

God is neutral

What became so obviously clear to me by the Holy Spirit as I studied this verse is that, in effect, Jesus was teaching that God is neutral concerning our need. Although He loves us with an incomprehensible love, still it is up to **us** to posture ourselves to 'pull' from His presence. The widow did not casually or nonchalantly ask the judge to help her. She persisted. Her persistence must have been a sight to behold, because the judge, in his mind, made a decision, saying to himself that even though he didn't fear God or man, and he basically didn't care what anyone thought, he answered her because she would not let him alone.

Again, although God loves us, and has made awesome provision for each of us, what we receive is often going to be because of the level of **our** persistence and desire.

God is neutral in the sense that He leaves it up to us. But He is a rewarder of those who diligently (not casually) seek Him (Hebrews 11:6).

An example of putting a demand on God

The following story demonstrates 'faith working through love' when a word of knowledge was delivered through the Holy Spirit in a church meeting in Kansas City. Eleven people, including the recipient's wife, said, 'That is God's word for Terry.' At that precise time, he was in critical condition at a local hospital. Sovereignly, God not only healed Terry's diabetes, but God moved **perpetually**, healing several other serious conditions he also suffered with – high blood pressure, high cholesterol, and even a severe athelete's foot condition.

Here is Terry Perkin's story.

Just before the Memorial Day Weekend, my daughter told me I looked like I was losing weight. I hadn't been feeling good, but I thought it was from the ulcer medicine I was taking. I went to a gastro-intestinal doctor, and upon doing a blood test, he told me my blood sugar was out of sight. He sent me to a diabetic specialist. My sugar was around 500 and I was told I had ketones – a fatty substance that gets into your bloodstream, a condition that caused anything I ate to turn to sugar. I had lost 36 pounds – basically I was starving to death. Because this was a life-threatening condition, I was instructed by the doctors to not return home, but immediately proceed to the hospital. I was officially diagnosed with type 1 Juvenile diabetes, which is very rare for an adult. Adults more commonly contract type 2, which can be controlled by diet or medicine.

I spent two weeks in the hospital, being given massive dosages of insulin. I had to learn to administer my own insulin shots.

At this time, Steve Sampson was in town for a series of meetings. At one of the meetings there was a word of knowledge that someone in the congregation had diabetes. 'The Lord is going to heal you, but it will be gradual over a period of time.'

A number of people in the church knew of my condition and that I was in the hospital. Eleven people sent word to me that God had given a word just for me. I just remember saying, 'Praise Gŏd, I believe that.'

After two weeks, I was released, but it was necessary to go back every week for a checkup. The condition had worsened to a state at that point that I was unable to drive. My vision was terrible almost to the point of blindness and I couldn't recognize people four feet away. I had multiple symptoms – a heavy feeling like walking in concrete, constant cotton-mouth, I could hardly talk and had constant urination. I continued the weekly visits, and progressively started to get better. Finally I went in for a routine visit. The doctor called me into his office and said 'I've got something to tell you. You're not going to believe this. I have been cutting back the insulin dosage. Not only do you not have to take the shots anymore, you don't have to take oral insulin. Your blood sugar is normal.' Continuing on with the good news, the doctor stated, 'You don't have to take any more blood pressure medicine. Your blood pressure is normal.' (I had been on blood pressure medicine for ten years). 'Besides that you don't have to take your cholesterol medicine any more. It is normal.' (I had been on this medication for eight years.) Praise God.

(I asked Terry what his doctor thought about the miracle.)

Dr. Rosen, is a Jewish doctor from the Helman clinic which is known around the world. He was dry and matter of fact when I told him the testimony. He put me back in the hospital to check out the ulcers (diabetes really works on ulcers). He couldn't find the ulcer . . . it was gone! About six months later, I realized that my severe athlete's foot condition was totally cleared up. I had a serious case of athlete's foot for most of my life.'

The Lord gave me a scripture through this:

'He sent His word and healed them ...
declaring it and rejoicing.'   (Psalm 107:20–22)

I have had so many opportunities to share this testimony – telling it multiple hundreds of times. I work in a large factory setting – usually 600–700 people around me all the time. I tell everyone I can. To God be the glory!

Chapter 8

God Will Perform His Word

'So shall My word be that goes forth from My mouth; It shall not return to Me void, but it shall accomplish what I please, and it shall prosper in the thing for which I sent it.'

(Isaiah 55:11)

I stood at the luggage carousel at the Dallas–Fort Worth International Airport waiting for my bags to appear. Others stood around as well, frustrated that their bags hadn't arrived either. I had arranged my schedule to fly into Dallas from Chicago, and synchronized it so my wife's flight, coming in from Birmingham would land at approximately the same time. Realizing my wife's flight had probably arrived, I decided to walk the fifteen gates to where her flight was arriving to meet her.

Several minutes later I arrived at her gate and there she stood, her bags already in hand. 'Where is your luggage?' she asked. 'I don't know,' I replied, 'It didn't show up.' Then she said, 'They probably can't get the baggage compartment open on the plane.' I thought to myself, 'What a ridiculous statement to make. How did we ever end up together anyway?'

We proceeded down the corridor back to the gate where my plane had originally arrived. As we approached the gate, numerous people were still standing around, and the luggage carousel was still turning, but devoid of luggage. Just then, a voice came over the PA system, 'Those arriving on flight #343 from Chicago, we have good news and bad news.' The announcer continued, 'The good news is that your luggage is here; the bad news is we can't get the baggage compartment unlocked on the plane.'

I was in awe at the accuracy of the words my wife had spoken. She thought she was just making a flippant comment, yet what came out of her mouth was prophetic. The door was indeed jammed on the plane. The prophetic realm is so close and such a reality. The voice of the Lord is as close to us as our own breath. We can speak prophetically, and not even realize it. This is the reality of the New Covenant – the Holy Spirit lives within us.

Can God be trusted?

On four occasions God's people accused Him of strategizing to kill them.

At the edge of the Red Sea, with Pharoah's army in pursuit, the people rose up and said,

> 'Because there were no graves in Egypt, have you taken us away **to die in the wilderness?** Why have you so dealt with us, to bring us up out of Egypt? Is not this the word that we told you in Egypt, saying, "Let us alone that we may serve the Egyptians? For it would have been better for us to serve the Egyptians than that **we should die in the wilderness.**"' (Exodus 14:11–12)

Then at the Wilderness of Sin, hardly forty days out of Egypt they complained because of their hunger, saying,

> 'And the children of Israel said to them, "Oh, that we had died by the hand of the Lord in the land of Egypt, when we sat by the pots of meat and when we ate bread to the full! **For you have brought us out into this wilderness to kill this whole assembly with hunger.**"' (Exodus 16:3)

As they continued on their journey, they camped at Rephidim, this time complaining because of their thirst, saying,

> 'And the people thirsted there for water, and the people complained against Moses, and said, "**Why is it you have**

> *brought us up out of Egypt, to kill us and our children and our livestock with thirst?"'*   (Exodus 17:3)

On yet another occasion the king of Moab had decided to attack the king of Israel, and so the King of Judah, and the king of Edom joined forces with the king of Israel against Moab. When they realized there was no water for the army or for the animals, the king of Israel said,

> *'Alas! For the Lord has called these three kings together to deliver them into the hand of Moab.'*
> (2 Kings 3:10)

In each of these situations, God's promise was still valid, although circumstances had temporarily changed. Human nature, in a state of panic, immediately accused God of abandonment and murder.

God doesn't change His mind or go back on His word

On my wife's thirty-second birthday, she was on her way to a meeting at the church where we pastored, when suddenly, she heard the Holy Spirit speaking to her, 'Your thirty-second year is going to be a monumental year.' She was so ecstatic as she related to me what the Lord had declared to her. So was I. We just knew all kinds of things were going to transpire immediately. Yet for the next forty-nine weeks, absolutely nothing out of the ordinary took place.

Then just three weeks before her thirty-third birthday, I had a visitation from the Lord in the middle of the night, wherein He instructed us to resign our pastorate, specifically saying to me, 'I want you to leave your comfortable place and take a giant leap of faith.' We immediately obeyed and resigned our eight-year pastorate the following Sunday. Also during those last few weeks of my wife's thirty-second year, she was sovereignly blessed with a major physical breakthrough in her body, which was a monumental blessing, as the Lord had told her nearly fifty-two weeks previously.

During that entire year, we were challenged to believe the word, although nothing seemed to be happening that we could see with our natural senses.

God doesn't forget you

A year later, through a series of miraculous events, we were directed by the Lord to move from Texas to Alabama. Over a number of months, God had spoken to us in a variety of ways. He confirmed to us again and again He was indeed moving us to live in Birmingham, Alabama. The first of September, we took our children and all our belongings on the journey to Alabama, making the giant leap of faith God had told us to take. It was exhausting, but adventurous. We **knew** we were moving in the will of God.

But after we arrived in Birmingham, and were unpacking our things in a rented apartment, I was severely attacked by fear. All kinds of thoughts barraged my mind. We did not know one person in this 'new' city. We had no local church contact. Our children knew no one. No one even knew we were in Birmingham except God. We did finally meet a realtor, but that was all. Even in the grocery store, I felt like approaching people asking them to be my friend. Finally one evening I 'begged' the Lord to please speak to me again, as I was overwhelmed with the thought that I had not heard God at all, but had done something crazy. I call this 'obeyer's remorse'.

That night I had a dream. In the dream I was perched and bouncing on a huge red rubber ball – like toy stores sell for toddlers. The Holy Spirit spoke to me in poetry, 'You just keep bouncing along, and you know it won't be long, that I'll open a door for you, and you'll go right on through.'

Here I was living in a state of panic, battling fear – yet the Holy Spirit is of course unmoved, showing me bouncing on a rubber ball.

Within a short time, God was true to His word. He opened doors upon doors and proved over and over His faithfulness – by introducing us to many new people and contacts we never dreamed of having.

A friend of ours, Pat Parks, a minister from Arkansas, was in a battle in her mind, dreading turning fifty years old. She didn't know why, but she couldn't get peace about reaching this point in her life. But on the morning of her fiftieth birthday, the instant she came out of sleep, the Spirit of God was speaking to her in rap! He said,

'This is your year of jubilee,
For the Lord Your God has set you free,
So look up My child, and begin to rejoice,
For you've just heard your Master's voice.'

Pat is a dignified-acting person and has never spoken in rap before this incident. Yet God (who has a great sense of humor), was unmoved by her stress and spoke to her in this unconventional manner. In the following years, Pat has been used by God to minister in many unusual ways. There have been unique occasions in her life where the anointing of God would move on her and she would begin to preach in rap. Don't ask me why. This has proven to be a very effective and anointed ministry 'tool' for her. I do know we can't put Him in a box.

The end of the Lord

Since God cannot lie, and He has promised to fulfill His word, sometimes we have no choice but to simply stand on His word.

'... *having done all, to stand.'*   (Ephesians 6:13)

*'Indeed, we count them blessed who endure. You have heard of the perseverance of Job and seen the **end intended** by the Lord – that the Lord is very compassionate and merciful.'*
(James 5:11)

God's intention is to always bring us through – not to leave us in the midst of a trial. The end of the Lord is good!

God is faithful to His word

Very recently I received a call from an excited pastor giving me a wonderful report. Five years ago I spoke prophetically to a children's teacher in her church. The word given was that this teacher would be used by God as a missionary, although she wouldn't necessarily relocate to a certain country. After that time, the little church went through a severe testing. There would rarely be children present in the little Sunday School. However, the pastor and these teachers felt the Lord tell them just to be faithful. So week after week they prepared quality lessons anyway, and Sunday after Sunday there would be no children to teach. Finally, things began to change and they were thrilled to finally be teaching children their Holy Spirit inspired curriculum. They soon came to the realization what God had given them to teach over those months of childless classes was very anointed, and they felt led by God to video tape the sessions. The tapes revealed Holy Spirit inspired remarkable events, including (among other things) very small children who had memorized large portions of Scripture.

When the pastor called me, she was so excited explaining that her sister had recently traveled to the Philippines, taking the video tape with her. The tape was shown to nearly 5000 children and greatly influenced them. A Christian man involved in teaching the children was given a daily hour of television time, and he felt strongly led to put the video on national television thereby having an impact on the nation.

God knows how to fulfill His word and you and I can rest in confidence that He will bring it to pass. It is not always as we think it should be, or even in the time frame we want it to occur – but it will always come to pass.

Last year, a retired pastor called me explaining, 'You probably don't remember me, but I was previously a pastor in New York and fifteen years ago, you ministered in my church for one evening.' As he continued speaking, I faintly recollected the incident. 'Anyway,' he continued, 'I live in your city now and am retired.' 'Tomorrow,' he said, 'a woman who was in my church when you happened to be there is traveling through and I want you to meet her.' He went on to explain that while I was ministering under the unction of the Spirit in his church that night, he knew that most of the people had never been exposed to the prophetic gifts. After I had preached, the Spirit had moved on me to pray over certain people. This particular lady was frozen with fear, as she had never experienced anything like this. She prayed to the Lord, 'Whatever You do, keep him from praying over me.' Well, the Lord honored her prayer and I never prayed over her, but as I was walking past her, I said (prophetically) 'There is a woman here to whom God is going to give a child.' She said that her friend next to her stated, 'Oh God, I hope it is not I.' Then this woman said, 'Oh, that could never be.' She and her husband had been told by medical doctors that they could never have children.

It wasn't more than a few weeks following that Monday evening meeting, that this lady realized she was pregnant. The pastor wanted me to meet this precious lady and introduced me to her fourteen-year-old son. Needless to say, it was a real joy to meet her and her son, whom God obviously has His hand on mightily.

Warring over the word

A friend of mine who has a wonderful ministry to the inner city youth, called me on New Year's Eve. He said, 'Steve, my wife and I are on our way to church to usher in the new year, but I just had to tell you what happened.' He related to me how in May he was in a home meeting one morning where I was speaking. At one point, the word of the Lord came to him through prophecy, saying, 'This is your year for break-through. Even if nothing happens till the last day of the year, don't forget – this is your year.'

He acquired a copy of the tape of the prophetic word spoken over him that day. Over the phone that night, he told me, 'Steve, I played the tape every single day since May, "reminding" the Lord of what He said.' His voice shook with excitement as he continued, 'Yesterday, December 30th, a man walked up to me and handed me the keys to a building. He told me that he was giving me the building for my ministry.' We rejoiced together, giving God the glory.

Our friend was a perfect example of what God requires of us. Although God had made the promise to him, he still realized it was his responsibility to embrace the word and fight off the doubts of the enemy.

When God was cutting the Covenant with Abram, vultures came to devour the sacrifice, but it plainly says that Abram (not God), drove the vultures away.

> *'And when the vultures came down on the carcasses, **Abram** drove them away.'*   (Genesis 15:11)

Likewise, Paul instructed his son in the faith, Timothy, to be aggressive in warfare concerning the prophetic promise over his life.

> *'This charge I commit to you, son Timothy, according to the **prophecies previously made** concerning you, that **by them you may wage the good warfare.'***   (1 Timothy 1:18)

Again, Paul exhorted Timothy, who may have had a problem being timid or passive,

> *'**Do not neglect the gift** that is in you, which was **given to you by prophecy** with the laying on of the hands of the eldership.'*   (1 Timothy 4:14)

> *'Therefore I remind you to **stir up** the gift of God which is in you through the laying on of my hands. For God has not given us a spirit of fear, but of power and of love and of a sound mind.'*   (2 Timothy 1:7)

God will not necessarily stir us up. That is our responsibility. But God will maintain His commitment to bring a performance of His word in our lives.

The creative word vs the Internal Revenue Service?

While ministering in Indianapolis one evening, there was an anticipation in the air – a sense that anything was possible. Suddenly the Holy Spirit spoke that there was someone present who had been in a battle with the Internal Revenue Service. A couple present, Dan and Doris, immediately jumped up from their seats, saying 'That's us!' Everyone knew that God was moving mightily and we prayed a prayer, receiving and accepting this wonderful oracle and promise from God. Then the Holy Spirit spoke specifically to them, 'There will be an immediate breakthrough and it will be settled in your favor.'

Ten years previously, Dan and Doris had a major house fire. There house was a total loss, and all their belongings had perished in the fire. The problem with the Internal Revenue Service began when they simply reported the loss on their tax return. For ten years, the government kept demanding that they owed money; so their accountant re-filed their tax return at least once a year for ten years. Not only did the government demand that they repay the money that they rightfully did not owe them, but they also demanded the penalty and interest reimbursement as well.

Within a few days of the meeting when God gave them that word, they received an unexpected letter from the Internal Revenue Service, telling them their amended return (of ten years) was being reevaluated and considered for validation. The letter declared that if it was indeed valided, they would receive a specified amount of money **with interest**. Two weeks from the time of the meeting when the Holy Spirit spoke that word, Dan and Doris had the government check in hand. They were not only reimbursed for the full amount of the loss they originally filed, but additionally for ten years of interest!

God watches over His word.

Yes, God will perform His word

The following is a testimony showing God's unique provision and His faithfulness to perform His word. Kevin's willingness to embrace God with childlike faith was greatly rewarded.

In 1994, I came to a meeting in Loogootee, Indiana. Having been unemployed for eight months, I was desperate for a word from God about a job, as we were quickly closing in on bankruptcy. During the meeting I kept calling out to God for 'my' word, but no word came. Then Steve Sampson had a word that God was going to heal back problems and instructed everyone who needed his back healed to come forward.

I had injured my back 17 years earlier on a trampoline, but had grown accustomed to the pain. I thought to myself, 'This is for someone else, my back is not **that** bad!' and 'These other people are the ones who need it more than I do, and besides, I came for a word about my job.' My back pain had stopped me from working or exercising in the past, and deep down I knew that I was going to require medical attention soon. But in **my mind**, I needed a word about a job.

Suddenly, I said to myself, '**Wait a second,** if God is going to heal backs, then I'm going to get in on the blessing. I may have come to hear about my job, but I need this too.' So I went forward and waited with the other twenty people who had already responded. Then Steve touched my back in the spot where it was injured and said, 'Father, I thank you for correcting this thing in my brother's back,' and then he began ministering to someone else.

I felt no jolt, nor spark; I felt nothing. But I did hear the Lord say to me, 'Bend forward, bend right, bend left.' I did as I heard, yet felt nothing different. At this time Steve came back to me and began to prophesy about my job to this effect, 'Brother, God is going to open up the door for you in something employment-wise; it is going to be your heart's desire, for God is doing something to get you a job that will **meet your needs.**'

I thought I needed a job, but God knew what I **really** needed. My agenda was not complete, but God's always is.

Thank God for the healing, because I really needed it as a faith-builder over the next four months. I began the next day to notice what seemed like two rods inserted in my back, supporting me where the injury had been. At once I noticed that I could move better, and the pain was gone. But, no job. It took four months longer until General Electric finally called me. But praise God, they did and my new job pays more than twice the amount of any job I had ever had.

Kevin Andry, Bedford, Indiana

Chapter 9

Yes, But Does the Spirit Move?

> *'Now the Lord is the Spirit; and where the Spirit of the Lord is* (where the Spirit is Lord), *there is liberty.'*
>
> (2 Corinthians 3:17)

On my first trip to the famous Toronto Airport Church in Toronto, Canada I was amazed at the crowd that filled the building that weekend. The presence of the Lord was so strong it was impossible to describe. I obediently did what a number of people counseled me to do, 'If you go, whatever you do, get to the front and get prayed for.' There were so many testimonies of lives changed and churches radically transformed by the impartation of the Holy Spirit through what God was doing there.

However, as I stood in line with scores of other people desiring prayer, it seemed that all those designated to pray passed me by again and again. Finally, after what seemed to be an eternity, two boys about ten years old approached me. Looking up at me, they asked, 'Sir, would you like prayer?' Everything in me wanted to reply, 'Yes, but not from you.' But I knew better, so I acknowledged that I did indeed desire prayer. Immediately they both reached up, putting their hands on me as high as they could reach, and one of them began to pray in a passionate, but tender tone. On and on he prayed. To my amazement, he verbalized each and every detail I had discussed with the Lord on my way to Toronto. He prayed about things in my past, and prayed about things yet to come that God had already written on my heart. The one boy, obviously the other's 'assistant', didn't pray but it was plain he was in total fervent agreement. After this lengthy prayer session, they both looked up at my blank face and innocently asked, 'Would there be anything else?' I replied, 'No, that just about covers it.' They each gave me a hug and walked away looking for someone else who wanted prayer. As I went back to my seat, I shook my head in awe at how God revealed His love for me through these two young boys. Truly there is no age in the realm of the Spirit – it is all God. The next day I realized that the back pain I had carried for a long time was completely gone and has never returned.

The bottom line

I have only one question when people begin to tell me about the church they are enthused about. My question is simple and forthright. 'Is the Spirit allowed to move in your midst?'

Two problems that seem to be pivotal issues concerning whether or not a church truly moves in God, are control and human respect. Church after church blessed with increase, so often turn to the same bondage – that of compromising the willingness to let the Spirit have freedom to move as He wills.

It is heartwarming to behold a new church in progress. Excited believers in earnest prayer, seeking continual daily guidance from the Holy Spirit. Often their initial meetings begin in a humble store-front or rented building where space is cramped, chairs are uncomfortable and the acoustics are poor. Many relate similar experiences of the months and even years of tedious routines of setting up chairs and moving heavy equipment for each meeting; as often the space they rent is also rented to other groups. The music is usually less than first quality, but it is pure. By pure, I mean, that although there may be a lack of talent, and the sound system is less than adequate, the worship is from the heart. There is no concern about who is present, for all hearts are in fervent passion toward the Lord.

I've witnessed church after church in these glorious, yet humble beginnings, experience the blessings and increase of God. More people attend. The finances increase. A building fund is started. Time flies, and before you know it, an excited assemblage of saints consecrate their new building to the

Lord. Everyone admires the new meeting place, the new padded chairs, the new carpet, the spacious platform, the awesome sound system, the ample parking, and the list goes on.

But all too frequently something else changes. The pure and childlike responsiveness to the Spirit begins to occur less and less. And sadly, things become predictable. The order of each meeting is painfully foreseen by all. Instead of spontaneity, the meetings become regimented and boring. Professionalism takes over. The music is perfect, the songs are flawless, but the presence of the Lord is ominously missing.

Human respect

The fear of man and the uncrucified desire to please people have the most diabolical effect on the church. Desiring to reach new souls, human nature strives to make things palatable and non-offensive. However, when the church was small and struggling, no one seemed to care what anyone thought. But now, all effort is focused on offending no one. Special care is made not to sing too long, stand too long, pray too long, and in general an attitude develops of toning down everything in order to keep it 'palatable'. As Jesus said,

> *'They loved the praises of men more than the praise of God.'*
> (John 12:43)

When you think about it, what do we have to offer any person but the flow of the Spirit? What I've asked God for continually is that He only send me to hungry people. How frustrating it is to minister to someone who is not hungry. What a waste of time and energy.

To any church, I want to challenge those in leadership to realize the reason people come through your doors is because they are hungry for the move of the Holy Spirit. They are looking for the real – the uncompromised Gospel. So many of the churches that began in a flow of purity have sadly reached (or fallen to) a level of mediocrity, which is becoming more and more common. It is almost like an unspoken formula. Many cities are full of churches (including charismatic) that have succumbed to a palatable man-pleasing Gospel. But any person who truly is hungry for more of God, will never be satisfied until experiencing the true flow of the Holy Spirit.

What are the benefits of yielding to the Spirit?

When my wife and I pastored a nondenominational church in Texas, by the grace of God we experienced an innocent and fervent desire to see God move in every service. Because we had graciously tasted an abundant moving of the Holy Spirit in the beginning years of our walk with God, we remained hungry for more. Therefore, we encouraged people to yield to what the Spirit gave them. We knew this was a risk, because there will always be people who yield to their flesh. But we also understood that people can only grow by **doing**.

The gifts of the Spirit must be **exercised** in the lives of Christians in order for God's people to become more sensitive and accurate. We felt strongly that the Lord wanted people to exercise their spiritual gifts. Furthermore, the Holy Spirit showed us two things. One, that we were to see the local church as a classroom. People have to grow – so what better place to have the freedom to exercise and make mistakes than in the midst of God's people? If you can't test your wings in your spiritual gift of prophecy among your fellow believers, where can you exercise it? Two, that we were to 'see' each and every person as a 'minister'. Obviously, not all are called to the five-fold ministry, or to stand behind a pulpit, but every believer is called to minister the Good News, and can be equipped and operate in the gifts of the Spirit in his life.

During this time of pastoring it was so exciting because we encouraged each person to always obey the Holy Spirit, if God gave him a word. We based this on Paul's letter to the Corinthians, specifically:

> *'How is it then, brethren? Whenever you come together, each of you has a psalm, has a teaching, has a tongue, has a*

> *revelation, has an interpretation. Let all things be done for*
> *edification.'*   (1 Corinthians 14:26)

As people yielded to the Lord, my wife and I would stand in awe, as in practically every meeting there would be a number of prophetic words come forth from our congregants that would literally foretell the entire premise of what I had prepared to teach. No one had any way of knowing what I had prepared in private through prayer and study. Truly God was glorified. Often, the most accurate word would come through those who seemed 'insignificant' in some people's eyes (not God's). But even though the person giving the word was not called to a position of leadership, there was no doubt the prophetic word was straight from God.

Once people were given the opportunity to exercise their gift and to 'step into the river' of God, it was amazing how quickly they **grew**. Not only did their spiritual gifts become more accurate, but their spiritual hunger and desire grew mightily. We knew this was because they thrived on the encouragement that they were indeed hearing the voice of God, and were permitted to yield to what they received.

This is not to say that there were never problems with fleshly manifestations. Sure there were those who gave forth words that made no sense or were extremely shallow. And there were a few occasions when people tried to take over the service, because they were 'in tune with God'. We simply had to pull those few aside and gently try to correct them, explaining that God does not interrupt Himself by doing two things at once. Yes, we had to deal with the rebellious nature of people, but the growth in the majority far outweighed the few 'displays' of flesh from the minority.

But in general people want to know how to hear from God, and that kind of growth comes by **doing**. People grow quickly when they begin to hear the Lord. One way to illustrate this, is when people start out yielding to God, they may give forth a mixture of Spirit and flesh. One may give forth a word that is 60% God and 40% flesh, but as he continues to exercise the gift, it will grow to 80% God and 20% flesh, and so forth. One has to start somewhere, and there is always room to make mistakes as long as there is a teachable spirit.

Spiritual growth occurs, not when the brain learns more facts about the Bible (which is good), but when the spirit of a person begins to experience the river of God flowing through him.

> *'...out of his heart will flow rivers of living water.'*
> (John 7:38)

Don't shut God down

The travesty in the New Testament church, which is far too common, is with leaders who have had a few bad experiences with people functioning in the spiritual gifts, but who have actually yielded to their flesh. Their way of solving the problem is to simply shut the Holy Spirit down, giving unspoken (sometimes spoken) rules that, 'We don't want anyone giving out a message from the Lord.'

Recently I was in a service with a very well-known pastor. A large portion of his message was devoted to telling of his experience with someone who had prophesied to him and to others, what he didn't perceive as being from God. I could agree with the pastor that the person might well have been wrong, unstable, and out of order. But this pastor (who believes in the gift of prophecy) gave a passionate thirty-minute discourse strongly implying that nearly anyone who ever gives out a word is a wolf and should be quickly exposed. I am well aware that correction is sometimes needed, and indeed we have to be on the lookout for 'wolves', but they are in the minority. I couldn't believe my ears as the pastor bluntly encouraged no one to prophesy at any time. Sadly, two thousand people were present, and you could 'hear' all of them saying to themselves, 'You'll never catch me ever yielding to prophecy regardless of the Holy Spirit's prompting.'

But what about the Scripture?

> *'Pursue love, and **desire** spiritual gifts, **but especially that you may prophesy.**'* (1 Corinthians 14:1)

And,

> *'But he who prophesies speaks* **edification and exhortation
> and comfort** *to men.'*   (1 Corinthians 14:3)

God seems to put an extremely high premium on the gifts of the Spirit which build up the body of Christ, and so should we.

Just because we may have run into false (or erroneous) teaching, doesn't mean we shut out all **teachers**, any more than if we came across a counterfeit twenty dollar bill, we refused to spend money any more.

The Holy Spirit is a sensitive Person. He will not force Himself on anyone and will not manifest in the creative realm where He is not welcomed nor received.

Discouraging the flow of the gifts is like telling God we never want the creative word spoken here again, unless its through the 'leadership'. Actually this position is saying we really don't trust the other 'joints' to supply.

> *'From whom the* **whole body**, *joined and knit together by what* **every** *joint supplies, according to the effective working by which* **every part does its share**, *causes the growth of the body for the edifying of itself in love.'*   (Ephesians 4:16)

In no way do I believe it is scriptural to reduce certain members of the body to only be 'capable' of menial tasks, or helps ministries. All members should be growing in their capacity to hear the Lord. That doesn't mean, just because someone is sensitive to the Lord, he should automatically be in leadership. But God said,

> *'All shall* **know Me**, *from the least of them to the greatest of them.'*   (Hebrews 8:11)

I have been in churches where I was appalled at the lack of maturity in the people. It definitely wasn't due to not having heard enough teaching or preaching. It is more than likely a by-product of leaders who are insecure, controlling and paranoid about embracing any other expression in the body of Christ, besides the ones that parrot everything they themselves believe. It is a narrow-minded concept of isolating particular bodies of believers to the 'one stream' mentality which produces stunted growth. God will never give all truth to one segment of the body of Christ. No one eats only potatoes every meal. There are giftings in the body we have been cheated out of experiencing because of the extreme control in leadership.

Who's out of order?

During the years we pastored, we experienced persecution from other charismatic churches. As we had encouraged people to yield to the Spirit, word traveled fast. One of the sharp criticisms that quickly came to our ears was that our church was in error because we had **more** than three prophecies per service. I assumed that they based their criticism from Paul's instruction to the Corinthian church,

> *'If anyone speaks in a tongue, let there be two, or at the most three, each in turn, and let one interpret.'*
> (1 Corinthians 14:27)

Although this criticism hurt, and yes, at times there were more than three prophecies in one service (sometimes four), I knew we were moving in the Holy Spirit, by giving people the opportunity to exercise in the Spirit.

However, this troubled me a lot; no one likes to be criticized. So I went to the Lord about it. I asked the Lord, 'What about this? What should I say to this kind of criticism that we have too much tongues and prophecy?' The Lord said to me, '**Tell them that they are in error because they don't have any.**'

It always amazes me that people would prefer to have nothing, than to take a risk and experience something.

It thundered!

It was a summer evening in June, 1995. I was conducting meetings at Evangelistic Church in Kansas City, Missouri. We had experienced a wonderful time in the presence of God for three days and we all knew our lives were forever changed. I so appreciate the pastor, Rev. John Crane, the grandson of the founder of the 50-year-old-church, who was sovereignly raised up by God a few years after his father died suddenly of a heart attack at age 47. What a heart for God this young man in his early thirties has! He has a heritage of a family of worshipping people who understand the extreme importance of listening to the voice of God, and letting the Spirit move and manifest Himself.

We left the last service that summer evening, and decided to stop at a restaurant before he took me back to my lodging. We pulled into the parking lot and as we got out of the car, I distinctly heard the Holy Spirit say, 'You'll be back here in six months.' As we walked into the restaurant, I told Pastor John what the Lord had spoken to me. 'Sure,' he said, 'you are welcome here anytime.' Neither of us recognized that God was talking about a divine appointment.

Months later, John called me. 'God has spoken to me,' he exclaimed. 'He told me that we are to have forty continuous days of meetings, and we're to call them "river" meetings.' He was excited yet apprehensive. Forty straight days was a long time to ask people to come, yet he knew he had heard from the Lord. 'Will you come the first five days?' he asked, telling me that he would have others coming in during the balance of the meetings. I agreed to come. It was only later that we remembered that the meetings that would begin the third day of January were exactly six months from the time the Holy Spirit had said, 'You'll be back here in six months.' Truly something was being birthed in the Spirit.

During those forty days (which went well beyond that duration) it was estimated that over 14,000 people came through the doors of Evangelistic Center Church and received prayer. Nothing has been the same since. The fresh breath of God has continually swept through that church since those forty days. Countless lives have been transformed by the power of God and hungry souls cry out for more.

The first night of the 'river' meetings there was intense resistance in the air, as some souls (specifically clergy) clearly only came to spectate. Discerning that the Spirit was being quenched by some present who were expecting a show, we closed the meeting early. The second night we felt a similar atmosphere. But not very long into the meeting, a small group of people got up and left. As soon as they walked out, all heaven broke loose in the place. Everyone felt the joy and freedom and began to celebrate. During this precious time, Pastor John Crane kept hearing thunder. At first he thought it was the church water pipes pounding. No – it was thunder. He whispered to a couple of elders to go outside to report on the storm. Their report was that the sky was clear. Following the meeting, several people approached him reporting that they had also heard thunder. One person present described the noise like the sound of many horses' hooves.

What have you got to lose?

Since those meetings, people continue to experience the awesome flow of the Holy Spirit at Evangelistic Center Church. The presence of the Lord became so intense in many of the meetings, a number of people were unable to stand up once they had been prayed for, and they fell to the floor. Following that holy manifestation, supernatural laughing would break out in the midst of the expectant people present. Naturally this power and laughter hit the pastor too, as he welcomed the outpouring of the Holy Spirit in his church. People who had been lukewarm and on the sidelines spiritually, were becoming recognizably on fire for God.

After this continued on for several weeks, a prominent man who had been a part of the church for a few years came to the pastor to complain. His statement was, 'I've watched the things that are happening, and I suppose it is okay, but since this laughter has started I've had a real problem with it.' He went on to say, 'My concept of holiness is that of a monk. It seems like God wants people quiet, not laughing with joy. Aren't you afraid of taking people astray?'

'Yes!' he replied, '**But I'm also afraid of taking people nowhere.**'

This man made it clear that if he were to stay, the pastor would have to tone things **way** down. So my friend sought the Lord. 'What shall I do about this?'

The Lord spoke to him, 'If you make him promises, you can keep him, but **he'll become your source.**' Thank God Pastor Crane heard the Lord and was strong enough to obey. The member with the 'problem' was a millionaire, and tithed a very generous amount to the church, somewhere equal to the giving of ten to twelve prosperous families. All this came at a time when they especially needed the financial support. This man's departure was the equivalent of losing many families. The pastor didn't back down and the man left.

However, months later a guest minister was moved on by the Holy Spirit to receive an offering to pay off the balance of the church mortgage. The mortgage was sizable, and this church in forty years of existence had never received a special offering for this type of need. But when the guest minister told the people that he was led of the Spirit to do so – in eleven short minutes the building was paid off, as the people responded to God.

Pride

The greatest hindrance to receiving from the Spirit is pride. Pride has its root in Satan, and is held up by the self-nature.

Because of pride, human nature craves to keep things in control. We want things predictable, nothing unusual, nothing unplanned, all to protect our pride.

But more than anything else, we want things to be non-offensive. God doesn't seem to carry the same concerns. In fact, it seems as though He goes out of His way to offend the pride of man.

> '*God **resists** the proud, but gives grace to the humble.*'
>
> (1 Peter 5:5)

He not only doesn't help the proud, He resists him!

Where many leaders miss it, is when they succumb to the **spirit of control** in order to make sure things don't get out of hand.

I look at it this way. Where there is spiritual growth there are going to be messes.

> *'Where no oxen are, the trough is clean; but much increase*
> *comes by the strength of an ox.'*   (Proverbs 14:4)

Jesus was never intimidated by the exposure of flesh through human nature. He knew it was inevitable, but He also knew that growth would be the by-product of spiritual exercise. The disciples certainly displayed their share of 'flesh', but once exhorted by Jesus, the lessons became valuable training engraved on their hearts and spirits.

If you are a perfectionist, and demand perfect, clean, and organized surroundings, then don't have children. Children won't let you!

You can't have it both ways! If you want no mess, then you probably won't have much flow of the Holy Spirit. Those who cannot tolerate dirty diapers (or vomit) and toys on the floor shouldn't have children. Pastors who can't tolerate people growing in God and trying their wings, will surrender to the spirit of control and build strong walls to keep people in the boundaries they have established. This method truly works, but no spiritual growth will be witnessed under these circumstances.

Out of your spirit, not out of your brain

Recently I had a dream about a church that had just moved into a beautiful new building. I experienced great disappointment in the dream as I became aware this particular church had lost **all** freedom in their worship (I was familiar with the church in the natural). Suddenly I jumped up and began to exhort them to get free. I knew I was speaking by the Spirit of God in the dream as I exhorted them with the words, 'Jesus said that out of your innermost being would flow rivers of living water...'. He didn't say, 'Out of your brain would come a familiar song.'

I woke up amazed at the sarcasm expressed by the Spirit of God. No matter how much the Bible talks about the release of the Holy Spirit, we **still** rely so heavily on the natural mind.

Sadly there is so much professionalism in the body of Christ, it seems apparent that most meetings would be just as 'successful' if the Holy Spirit never showed up. We've learned to preach, sing, exhort, and even have altar calls so skillfully, we don't even lean on the Spirit of God.

One excellent gage to measure how freely and to what degree the Spirit is moving, is to question how much of the same repetitious activity (preaching, singing, exhortations, and altar calls) would occur in many churches, if the Holy Spirit were not even attending!

One size fits all mentality

I believe a good way to describe certain ministers is this. They love crowds, but they don't like people. One of the greatest offenses in the body of Christ is where people are not treated as individuals, and everyone is lumped into one huge category. I don't believe this is the heart of Jesus. I believe He sees the uniqueness and individuality of each person.

There is nothing that irks me more than the ministers that are quickly ushered off after preaching, or laying hands on a few at the altar. How can anyone think he is so spiritual that he has to make a beeline to a waiting car or a private room?

It seems Jesus made Himself available to the people.

The blessings of God were not meant to paralyze us

Have you ever noticed how well you pray when there is a great need or crisis, and how your prayer life suffers when things are going well? It shouldn't have to be this way, but it seems as though it is the very blessings of God which stagnate us. What is it about human nature, when things are going well, the bills are paid, the health is good, and the marriage is in good shape – that we slide into passivity and nothingness toward God?

It doesn't have to be this way. We **can** seek Him just as much in good times as in bad.

It is no wonder it is expressed this way in the book of Proverbs,

> 'Remove falsehood and lies far from me; give me neither poverty or riches – Feed me with the food allotted to me;

lest I be full and deny You, *and say, "Who is the Lord...?"'*   (Proverbs 30:8–9)

David prayed, *'I'm poor and needy'* (Psalm 86:1). He was a millionaire at the time, but knew he was **always** in desperate need of God. And so are we.

Chapter 10

Are You Still Coveting Legs?

A family has a dog that has bitten the legs of several passers-by. Not wanting to deal with law suits, they put the dog in a large cage and, to be extra sure, put a large chain on his neck. Now the problem is solved externally, because no-one's legs are being bitten. However, although chained and confined within a fence, the dog is still coveting legs.

The dog hasn't changed at all, but has only been restrained. This is what the law does; it doesn't change us, it only restrains us. Although we are not committing the act of sin, our hearts are still filled with the desire to commit that which is not lawful. Paul (whose company I'm glad to be in), expressed the same frustration, as he found himself helpless in dealing with his old nature.

> *'For I know that in me (that is, in my flesh) nothing good dwells; for to will is present with me, but how to perform what is good I do not find. For the good that I will to do, I do not do; but the evil I will not to do, that I practice. Now if I do what I will not to do, it is no longer I who do it, but sin that dwells in me.'* (Romans 7:18–20)

How many times have we heard the scenario of a child who has grown up in a Christian environment, but then runs headlong into rebellion? The child's heart was never changed. Only the exterior pressure kept the child in line. When the gate was opened, it was obvious that the heart was never renewed and converted.

But God has made an awesome promise. He will change our heart.

> *'Then I will give them one heart, and I will put a new spirit within them, and take the stony heart out of their flesh, and give them a heart of flesh, that they may walk in My statutes and keep My judgments and do them; and they shall be My people, and I will be their God.'* (Ezekiel 11:19–20)

Look in the mirror

Everyone does it. We get out of bed in the morning, and go stand in front of the mirror. Talk about fighting depression! Few look their best in the morning. In fact, the mirror always gives us the same message – 'Get help!' The mirror tells us to comb our hair, shave or put on make-up. But guess what? That is all the mirror can do for us. It just informs us we're in trouble – we need help. We can't take the mirror off the wall and use it as a comb or to shave with or apply make-up.

The mirror represents the law. The law can't help us; it only reveals who we really are. The purpose of the law is to drive us to frustration and desperation. So recognizing our helplessness, we run to the One who has already fulfilled the law – Jesus. He didn't come to do away with the law, but to fulfill it – every jot and tittle of it (Matthew 5:17–18). But once He fulfilled it, He abolished it as a means of our obtaining righteousness. The law is a schoolmaster to lead us to Christ. He has become our righteousness. Our righteousness is established before God by our belief and trust in Jesus. Our faith is manifested by recognizing and receiving what He did on our behalf, as He not only lived without sin, but gave His life as the supreme sacrifice and shed His righteous blood for us.

> *'For He made Him who knew no sin to be sin for us, that we might become the righteousness of God in Him.'* (2 Corinthians 5:21)

The law can't help us

So many Christians who love God have a propensity to get into legalism because of their desire to please God. When man tries to please God on his own merit, he naturally gravitates to rules and regulations. The law was never intended to clean us up or make us righteous, but only to reveal to us our sin nature.

> *'For the law made nothing perfect...'*   (Hebrews 7:19)

Paul expressed his frustration with the law.

> *'What shall we say then? Is the law sin? Certainly not! On the contrary, I would not have known sin except through the law. For I would not have known covetousness unless the law had said, "You shall not covet."'*   (Romans 7:7)

> *'But sin, taking opportunity by the commandment, produced in me all manner of evil desire.'*   (Romans 7:8)

> *'For we know that the law is spiritual, but I am carnal, sold under sin. For what I am doing, I do not understand. For what I will to do, that I do not practice, but what I hate, that I do. If, then, I do what I will not to do, I agree with the law that it is good. But now, it is no longer I who do it, but sin that dwells in me.'*   (Romans 7:17)

The purpose of the Old Covenant

Therefore, the real purpose of the Old Covenant was to show us that we need a New Covenant. The Old Covenant failed, because it depended on man's faithfulness.

> *'Not according to the covenant that I made with their fathers in the day when I took them by the hand to lead them out of the land of Egypt; because they did not continue in My covenant, and I disregarded them, says the Lord.'*
> (Hebrews 8:9)

But the New Covenant is a heart covenant. God writes His will on our hearts, and Christ lives within us to fulfill the will of God. We don't have to search 'out there' because His will is already written on our hearts.

'For this is the covenant that I will make with the house of Israel after those days, says the Lord: I will put My laws in their mind and write them on their hearts; and I will be their God, and they shall be My people.'   (Hebrews 8:10)

This is a covenant of intimacy, in that God has captured our hearts and by His grace replaced our hearts of stone with hearts of flesh.

Two covenants

The Old Covenant word for covenant is *berith*, which means 'a cutting of covenant with blood'. It meant an end to an independent attitude, and living in a relationship with mutual possession of goods, and accepting strengths as well as weaknesses and debts. It meant the blood of the two in covenant would flow together, as the covenant Jonathan and David made together, which not only included a pledge to each other but also to their future unborn children (1 Samuel 18).

The New Covenant word for covenant is *diatheke*, which is 'an unequal covenant between God and man'. God has taken the initiative and called us to Himself.

'And you, being dead in your trespasses and the uncircumcision of your flesh, He has made alive together with Him, having forgiven you all trespasses, having wiped out the handwriting of requirements that was against us, which was contrary to us. He has taken it out of the way, having nailed it to the cross.'   (Colossians 2:13–14)

The unequal covenant is God pledging all His assets to us and receiving all our weaknesses and shortcomings in return. This is the Good News Covenant. He is not holding our sins against us, and He has pledged all that He is to us.

From rules to relationship

The Old Covenant was rooted in rules. The ten commandments were clear cut commands of do's and don'ts for a lifestyle acceptable to God. When Jesus arrived on the scene, He didn't come to do away with the Law (the rules) but to fulfill it.

> *'Do not think that I came to destroy the Law or the Prophets, I did not come to destroy, but to fulfill.'*   (Matthew 5:17)

Through Jesus, we have been called into relationship with God. No longer do we serve God out of fear, but out of love.

> *'You shall love the Lord your God with all your heart, with all your soul, and with all your strength, and with all your mind, and your neighbor as yourself.'*   (Luke 10:27)

It becomes a heart covenant – a relationship that far supersedes keeping rules. It is based on love, not fear and dread.

Now when I sin, it is no longer breaking a rule, it is violating a relationship. Since it is now a love relationship, hearts are involved, not just actions.

From actions to motives

The Old Covenant scrutinized our actions, but the New Covenant scrutinizes our motives. Under the Old Covenant, the believer's responsibility was just to keep his actions in line with the law. But the New Covenant, although filled with mercy, searches our motives continually.

> *'For the word of God is living and powerful, and sharper than any two-edged sword, piercing even to the division of soul and spirit, and of joints and marrow, and is a discerner of the thoughts and intents of the heart. And there is no creature hidden from His sight, but all things are naked and open to the eyes of Him to whom we must give account.'*
> (Hebrews 4:12–13)

Now it is not enough just to avoid sin and do the right actions. Instead, we have to keep our heart in line with His and walk openly before Him.

Jesus instructed the disciples,

> *'No longer do I call you servants, for a servant does not know what his master is doing; but I have called you friends, for all things that I heard from My Father I have made known to you.'*   (John 15:15)

Just as Jesus lived in relationship with the Father, He calls us into the same intimacy. We now live in a higher realm than servants, for we are His friends. When my children were small, I told them what to do and when to do it, but as they've grown older, my relationship with them has changed. No longer do I have to remind them to brush their teeth or clean their room; instead I can share my heart with them on an adult level.

From performance to response

A common problem amongst Christians is a mind set that attempts to gain God's acceptance by deeds of performance. Confusing religion with relationship, we often fall back into 'works' which is nothing more than man trying to please God and find acceptance through what we perceive as what God wants.

Many, if not most Christians, are still bound to performance, still trying to gain brownie points with God through their efforts. There is too much religion and Phariseeism in most of us that needs to be rooted out.

But God doesn't want our performance, He wants our response. No longer are we to live by our initiative, conjuring up actions or self-denials to please God. Now we are to desire to be sensitive to His initiative; to have eyes and ears dedicated to paying attention to the promptings and impulses of the Holy Spirit.

The Law says, don't do it; the New Covenant says, don't want to do it

When we read the ten commandments, they begin with:

> *'You shall have no other gods before me.'*   (Exodus 20:3)

But when we read as far as the tenth commandment, it concludes with an interesting word, 'covet'.

> *'You shall not covet your neighbor's house, you shall not covet your neighbor's wife, nor his male servant, nor his female servant, nor his ox, nor his donkey, nor anything that is your neighbors.'* (Exodus 20:17)

Coveting deals with the 'want to' or the 'intent of the heart'. Even under the Old Covenant, we see beginnings of the New Covenant. God begins to point us to the motives and intents of the heart, which He promises to 'replace'. Jeremiah said of the heart,

> *'The heart is deceitful above all things, and desperately wicked, who can know it? I, the Lord search the heart. I test the mind, even to give every man according to the fruit of his doings.'* (Jeremiah 17:9–10)

It is our hearts that covet. Only the Holy Spirit can reveal what's in our heart. Only God can change our heart. He promises to take the stony heart out.

> *'Then I will give them one heart, and I will put a new spirit within them, and take the stony heart out of their flesh, and give them a heart of flesh.'* (Ezekiel 11:19)

A whole new perspective

Because we are in relationship with God, we recognize that life functions beautifully if He is at the center of our heart and affections. Instead of living by rules, we now learn to be led by the Spirit. Rather than try to do things to get God to accept us, we rest in the knowledge that we are His. Plainly, we believe the Gospel.

Under the law, we had to do certain things. Now we get to choose. Instead of having to go to church – just try to keep me out of church! Under the Old Covenant we owed God our tithe, but under the New Covenant, He owns it all! The good news is that Jesus has fulfilled the law so that we can enjoy a relationship with God.

'I have come that they may have life, and that they may have it more abundantly (to the full).'   (John 10:10)

David spoke prophetically of the New Covenant, and the relationship with God that was in store for us.

'I am the Lord your God Who brought you out of the land of Egypt; open your mouth wide, and I will fill it.'
(Psalm 81:10)

God will put His words in our mouth for every situation as we live in intimacy with Him.

'But My people would not heed My voice, and Israel would have none of **Me.** *'*   (Psalm 81:11)

God has always wanted a relationship with His people based on them listening to His voice and wanting Him, not just what He can do.

'Oh, that My people would listen to Me, that Israel would walk in My ways! I would soon subdue their enemies, and turn My hand against their adversaries.' (Psalm 81:13–14)

God will deal with our enemies, if we will listen to Him and walk in His ways.

The problem of legalism

Praise God for the sweet Holy Spirit. He brings life to every one of us. The New Covenant is a relationship that God has called us into – not a set of rules and regulations.

Say, for example, that a small child is warned not to touch the stove, and he touches it anyway. Do you punish the child? No, you don't need to. The punishment for disobedience is built in. The child has burnt fingers! No need to punish him more. In fact, there is little danger of his touching the stove again.

The highest rule or law, is that of obedience to the Holy

Spirit which comes out of a relationship with God, not a rule-keeping religion.

Legalism comes in countless forms, always manifesting through those who feel they have a corner on the truth. For example, some feel a strong conviction about Christmas being a commercial if not pagan holiday. In particular they have a conviction that a Christmas tree is an idol and an abomination to God. If that is their conviction they are free to follow it, and should follow it.

> *'Do you have faith? Have it to yourself before God. Happy is he who does not condemn himself in what he approves. But he who doubts is condemned if he eats, because he does not eat from faith, for whatever is not from faith is sin.'*
>
> (Romans 14:22–23)

But legalism becomes deadly when the person with that conviction determines to put that conviction (law) on every other person.

Perhaps God has dealt with you about avoiding a certain food. Then don't eat it. But don't try to bring the whole world into your 'revelation'. Why? Because the blood of Jesus Christ has set us free from rules and regulations. Now we are under a higher law!

We have to live by a relationship with the King. We have to live responsibly, not hiding behind mere rules, but to live with an open and transparent heart before Him, obeying Him daily.

The New Covenant leaves us free – not to do our own thing – but to follow the Author. What is wrong for one person (even under the Holy Spirit's command), may not be wrong for the next person.

We are free! We are called to be free! But freedom is not to be abused, rather it gives us the opportunity to serve and be a blessing.

> *'For you, brethren, have been **called to liberty**, only do not use liberty as an opportunity for the flesh, but through love serve one another. For the law if fulfilled in one word, even in this: "You shall love your neighbor as yourself."'*
>
> (Galatians 5:13–14)

The idiot-proof Covenant

We can't mess up with the New Covenant because it is not conditional on human performance. The New Covenant cannot fail, because it is a covenant between God and Jesus. And our place is in Jesus. He has paid our debt.

We own what I call an idiot-proof camera. It functions flawlessly. I can't mess it up. When I load the film, I shove it in the slot and it automatically advances to the first frame. When I take a picture, it automatically focuses and even flashes if needed. Then it automatically advances to the next frame. When I've taken the last picture, it automatically rewinds, just in case I am stupid enough to try to take another picture. It is truly an idiot-proof camera!

The New Covenant is built by the Manufacturer the same way. It is idiot-proof. It works every time! Prayers are answered even when we don't feel worthy or if we've had a bad day. God is honoring His Covenant, not because of our performance, but because of the cutting of His supreme Covenant, the shedding of Jesus' blood.

It is a listening Covenant

The New Covenant is grounded and centered in listening. It works and functions as we listen to our Covenant-Partner – God.

We flow with God in relationship, letting Him rule in our hearts. Just as a child and parent are in relationship, they can simply ask and receive results.

No longer do we have to battle to feel worthy (although most of us do). As His children, we can know we are part of the family. No child goes to his mom and dad saying, 'I don't feel worthy to be a part of this family, will you consider giving me up for adoption?'

Even when an outsider, the Centurion, saw the power of the Covenant-Provider, he told Jesus that he did not need to come under his roof, but to just speak the word in order for his servant to be healed.

> 'Lord, do not trouble Yourself, for I am not worthy that You should enter under my roof. Therefore I did not even think

myself worthy to come to You. But say the word, and my
servant will be healed. For I also am a man under authority,
having soldiers under me. And I say to one, "Go," and he
goes, and to another, "Come," and he comes, and to my
servant, "Do this' and he does it."'   (Luke 7:6–8)

The centurion became aware of how the Covenant worked. Even as an outsider, he recognized the authority of Jesus Christ – that He was indeed God Himself. His understanding was so pristine, that Jesus made a remark that He never made about the Jews.

*'I say to you, I have not found such **great faith**, not even in*
Israel.'   (Luke 7:9)

Children help me understand the Covenant

Children inherently feel like they belong. They know they are a part of the family. They never worry about finances. A child never comes to dad and asks, 'How is your bank account?' Children assume that you as a parent have all the resources they will ever need. When my son was about five years old, we were in a store and, as usual, he was asking me to buy him something. I decided to try a new approach to his ever persistent requests and told him, 'I just don't have enough money for that.' 'Write a check,' he replied.

I often make the statement that the body of Christ is in good shape, in spite of only lacking one thing – we don't believe the Gospel! I say that because I meet so few people who really believe that they are worthy to receive from God. So many pray from the standpoint of an outsider or someone begging for something that they do not deserve to receive. But the good news of the Gospel is that we have been made worthy! Of course, this worthiness is not based on anything we have done, but only merited because of what has already been accomplished through the shed blood of Jesus Christ.

As Christians, we need to ask the Holy Spirit to personally envelop us with a sense of worthiness, that God truly is our Father, and we can come boldly before Him with our petitions, totally unashamed, to ask Him to meet even the smallest need that we have.

When my son was in fifth grade, he informed me that he owed around seven dollars to pay a fine for an overdue library book. At a rate of ten or fifteen cents a day, it had been buried somewhere for a long time. I chided him that it was his fault for not returning it himself and explained that he had acted irresponsibly. He looked at me unmoved. As far as he was concerned, I was still the source for his need, even though he had fallen short in his performance. That is the exciting truth about the New Covenant. It works! God does not answer prayer based on our performance, but upon His!

Jesus didn't pray for anyone – He spoke the word

Early in my Christian walk I became acquainted with an Englishman who told me of his experience with the late Smith Wigglesworth. The man had a severe limp from a war injury. He stood in a long line, waiting for the evangelist, Wigglesworth to pray for him. Finally it was his turn. When he stood before him, Wigglesworth gruffly said, 'What do you want?' He replied, 'My leg is crippled from a war injury.' Wigglesworth didn't pray for him, but rather pushed him along, and again gruffly spoke, 'You ought to be glad you can walk.' The Englishman walked away, angry and disappointed, thinking how much he hated preachers. But after taking several steps, he realized his leg was completely healed!

When I ponder this testimony, it is easy to recognize that the ministry of Smith Wigglesworth was based on an intimate relationship with God. The man was obviously healed because the Lord had spoken to the evangelist. It was not Wigglesworth's prayers but His relationship with God that brought the results.

Searching through the New Testament, we never see an instance of Jesus praying for people. He always ministered to them: giving life, deliverance and healing. But He never stood there praying for anyone. In fact, the only time He prayed was as He stood before the tomb of Lazarus. However, in that instance He defined His prayer, saying,

> *'Father, I thank you that **You have heard Me**. And I know that You always hear Me, but because of the people who are standing by I said this, that they may believe that You sent Me...'*   (John 11:41–42)

Over and over, He spoke the word to needy people. To the man with an infirmity of thirty-eight years, He said, *'Rise, take up your bed and walk'* (John 5:8). To a man with a dying son He commanded, *'Go your way, your son lives'* (John 4:50). To a blind man, He spit on the ground, made clay, put it on the man's eyes and told him, *'Go, wash in the pool of Siloam'* (John 9:7). He interrupted a man's funeral to say, *'Young man, I say to you, arise'* (Luke 7:14). To ten leprous men, He told them, *'Go, show yourselves to the priest'* (Luke 17:14).

Are we to pray for people?

Now consider this, He didn't tell you and me to pray for people. He commands us,

> *'Heal the sick, cleanse the lepers, raise the dead, cast out demons. Freely you have received, freely give.'*
> (Matthew 10:8)

What a truth! We have the goods to give. He didn't tell us to pray for people, but to **give** to them – give healing, give strength, give deliverance. Why? Because He lives in us.

When do we pray? We pray as Jesus did. He sought the Father early in the day, then went forth in might and power. We can live in His presence, seeking Him and staying built up in Him. Then when we encounter needs, we are ready to give forth.

Because we are in covenant with God, His virtue flows through us.

Therefore, when Jesus prayed at the tomb of Lazarus, He was able to pray, *'Father, I thank you that you **have** heard Me.'* It is obvious that He and the Father had conversed earlier about

Lazarus. No doubt the Father had already revealed to Jesus that Lazarus would be raised from the dead. When He stood at his tomb, it was just a matter of calling Lazarus to life, a matter that was already settled – a prayer that had already been heard.

Chapter 11

Choose Life!

- Jesus didn't go around making bad people good, He went around making dead people live.

- **Bitterness** – drinking poison, and hoping the other person will die.

Jesus didn't die to get us into heaven; Jesus died to get us into fellowship with God. When we make heaven the goal, we reduce salvation to a place. But salvation is not a place; salvation is a Person. It is not a system of beliefs or even a religion; far from it. Christianity is a **relationship** with the Founder, Leader, CEO, Boss, Lord, Author of the Covenant, and King of kings and Lord of lords. So often, we have heard that the only issue of salvation is heaven or hell. This is true in one sense, because heaven and hell are certainly conse-quences of salvation or the lack thereof. But salvation most accurately could be described as an issue of life or death.

> '*I call heaven and earth as witnesses today against you, that* **I have set before you life and death**, *blessing and cursing; therefore* **choose life**, *that both you and your descendants may live.*' (Deuteronomy 30:19)

God makes it easy. He not only shows us the choices, but tells us what choice to make. Choose life!

Growing up in a legalistic religious setting, I never under-stood why sincere Christians always made me feel bad, to the point of believing that I would never measure up. Sunday mornings always seemed to be an ongoing scenario of reviewing failures and anticipating defeats. Looking back, I realize these Christians were living from the tree of the knowledge of good and evil instead of the tree of life. Sincerely, yet in ignorance, people offered truth without love, correction without mercy, and condemnation instead of an escape to life and freedom.

When the Pharisees brought a woman to Jesus whom they had caught in the very act of adultery, both He and the Pharisees had the **same objective** in mind – to get her to stop sinning. But although they both had the same objective, they had two totally different outlooks. The Pharisees wanted to kill her (that stops sin every time), but Jesus wanted to deliver and release her. One offered death – the other offered life.

According to the law, they were correct; for the law, indeed, states that the penalty of sin is death. However, the good news of the Gospel is that Jesus is greater than the law and He came to fulfill the law and therefore offered life to her, and to you and me as well.

Jesus didn't come to do away with the law, but to fulfill it (Matthew 5:17) but once He fulfilled it, He abolished it as a means of making us righteous. Now righteousness does not come from our struggle to do right, but rather by receiving His righteousness in place of ours. Talk about good news – instead of condemnation and a life of failure and defeat, He tells us (as He told the woman caught in adultery) go and sin no more.

Two trees

When Eve was deceived by the serpent to eat of the tree of the knowledge of good and evil, with her husband's consent, the consequences were that their eyes were opened and they lost their innocence.

> '*So when the woman saw that the tree was good for food, that it was pleasant to the eyes, and a tree desirable to make one wise, she took of its fruit and ate. She also gave to her husband with her, and he ate.* **Then the eyes of both of**

them were opened, and they knew that they were naked; and they sewed fig leaves together and made themselves coverings.'   (Genesis 3:6–7)

Once their innocence was gone, they became judges. When we judge something, we then make a decision about our judgment and become victims of our judgment.

For example, if we are living from the tree of the knowledge of good and evil, and someone hurts or takes advantage of us, we naturally judge that as bad. Our judgment, then, becomes an all consuming desire to get even or to demand recompense from that person. However, if we are innocent (living from the tree of life) we are not judging the situation good or evil, but saying that it is in God's hands and God will turn it into good.

When we're the judge, we're always in trouble, because we see ourselves as the victim and our focus becomes centered on the one who hurt us.

In fact, once we've made the judgment, we usually cannot 'control' our resentment and anger and that person becomes the center of our focus, and in a sense, becomes the 'lord' of our life. No longer are we centered on the Lord, but on that person.

'Lest any root of bitterness springing up cause trouble, and by this many become defiled.'   (Hebrews 12:15)

Opportunity to minister life

When Paul and Silas cast an evil spirit of divination out of a slave girl, they were beaten and thrown into prison.

'Then the multitude rose up together against them; and the magistrates tore off their clothes and commanded them to be beaten with rods. And when they had laid many stripes on them, they threw them into prison, commanding the jailer to keep them securely. Having received such a charge, he put them into the inner prison and fastened their feet in the stocks.'   (Acts 16:22–24)

Paul and Silas had an opportunity to become bitter and to pray the wrath of God down upon the magistrates. Surely they would have felt justified in their feelings.

Instead, they chose to live from the tree of life. Rather than complain bitterly and gripe about their injustices, they plugged into life and began to sing! All the prisoners heard them singing. It seems like we'll always have an audience to see what tree we're eating from.

> *'But at midnight Paul and Silas were praying and singing hymns to God, and the prisoners were listening to them.'*
> (Acts 16:25)

Then God caused an earthquake. Our environment responds when we exalt the Lord. The earthquake was so mighty that the foundations of the prison were shaken and everyone's chains were loosed. Exalting God not only frees us, it frees others!

Now, if Paul and Silas were living from the tree of the knowledge of good and evil, they would have said, 'Let's make a run for it, these people are getting what they deserve.' But these wonderful men were plugged into the tree of life.

A man's life was at stake – the jailer who was commissioned to hold them securely. Only the Holy Spirit could have shown Paul that the jailer was going to kill himself, because it had to have been pitch dark in there. Paul was ministering life, and called out to the jailer not to kill himself.

> *'And the keeper of the prison, awaking from sleep and seeing the prison doors open, supposing the prisoners had fled, drew his sword and was about to kill himself. But Paul called with a loud voice, saying, "Do yourself no harm, for we are all here."'*
> (Acts 16:27–28)

The jailer, overwhelmed by this act of mercy, fell down at Paul and Silas's feet, saying, *'Sirs, what must I do to be saved?'* Of course, they led him and his family to Christ.

What a glory to God! They chose to continue to live from the tree of life, regardless of their adverse circumstances.

Life, not legalism

Although we want to obey God and minister life to others, many times we simply offer legalism. Take, for example, the doctrine of confession. Having a good confession as a Christian is certainly a wonderful truth. There are numerous scriptures regarding the need to have a good confession, such as 'Death and life are in the power of the tongue,' etc. There is no problem with this truth and it is certainly sound doctrine to have a good, positive and uplifting confession.

But the problem is that if we are still living from the tree of the knowledge of good and evil, we may have a right confession, but do it in is a spirit of legalism and condemnation. No longer are we offering people life, but rather putting them in bondage. In fact, every time we hear someone say something less than positive, we might come at them with a curt correction or a superior attitude – because living from that tree we see ourselves as a judge and not a life-giver.

James corrected those living from the wrong tree. The people were judging from the outward appearance and treating those who were nicely dressed and people of means, differently from those who may not have had as many possessions in this world.

> 'For if there should come into your assembly a man with gold rings, in fine apparel, and there should also come in a poor man in filthy clothes, and you pay attention to the one wearing the fine clothes and say to him, "You sit here in a good place," and say to the poor man, "You stand there," or, "Sit here at my footstool," **have you not shown partiality among yourselves, and become judges with evil thoughts** (motives)?'   (James 2:2–4)

Becoming a judge can be a dangerous thing – namely, because we are not **qualified** to judge. Judgment belongs to God. What are we supposed to do? We are to live as innocent children, leaving the judgment up to God. Any time I judge something outwardly, I am proved wrong. I am a poor judge. So are you. How many times have we acted like James and judged someone by the outward appearance, not recognizing the treasure that is in the person?

The issue is life

Often when God makes a truth known to us, we begin to 'minister' death. For example, perhaps someone has a strong conviction about reading large portions of the Bible daily. Then every time he meets someone who doesn't read the Bible frequently, he ministers death to him by saying something like, 'I can't believe you don't read your Bible more.' Although this person is doing something good, his attitude is from the tree of the knowledge of good and evil, and he is making a judgment against everyone he meets who isn't reading his Bible as much as he. If he were eating from the tree of life, he would proclaim something like, 'I can't believe the truths I am finding in this great book, something jumps out at me every day.' Or if God deals with us to pray more, immediately we want to condemn everyone who doesn't pray as much as we do.

Or, if God should deal with us about over eating, or driving over the speed limit, we often respond very quickly to lay a 'guilt trip' on others who have not been dealt with by God in that area. We minister death and the 'death sentence' permeates every area of our lives.

Innocence

When we live from the tree of life, we understand the Gospel. Jesus said we cannot enter the Kingdom unless we come as innocent children.

> 'Assuredly, I say to you, **unless you are converted and become as little children**, you will by no means enter the kingdom of heaven.' (Matthew 18:3)

Probably the reason that most people love little children is not only because they are cute, but that they are innocent and pure. They aren't 'smart' enough to become judges. They see the world through innocent eyes.

I would also point out that is why so many people love and enjoy pets, because the pet makes no judgment, he loves you unequivocally – just as you are.

Jesus talked a lot about innocence.

> *'Be wise as serpents, and harmless* (innocent) *as doves.'*
> (Matthew 10:16)

When the disciples were excited that the demons were subject to them, He exhorted them not to rejoice in that fact, but the fact that their names were written in heaven. Then He got excited and rejoiced greatly in the Spirit (which means to whirl around and dance), and said,

> *'I thank you, Father, Lord of heaven and earth, that you have* **hidden** *these things from the wise and prudent and* **revealed them to babes** (innocent). *Even so, Father, for so it seemed good in Your sight.'*   (Luke 10:21)

Jesus rejoiced over this truth, that in order to serve God, we must see everything through innocent eyes. It doesn't mean to be ignorant or stupid (be wise as serpents), but means that we cease to be judges (with all kinds of motives) and, instead, let God judge and control every situation – leaving the judgment to Him – living with complete and total trust.

We have to learn to continually choose life and maintain innocence.

> *'Keep* (watch over) *your heart with all diligence, for out of it spring the issues of life.'*   (Proverbs 4:23)

In order to stay plugged in to the tree of life, we have to keep a guard over our heart and not give in to bitterness or resentment. This is our responsibility, to 'protect' the life of God in us.

Cook or commune?

When Jesus was at the home of Martha along with her sister Mary, Martha was laboring in the kitchen. She was still living from the tree of the knowledge of good and evil. She had an agenda (not too innocent) to produce a whopper meal for Jesus. Since Mary wasn't giving her much assistance, she made a judgment that this was wrong. Immediately her anger was directed at Mary and even Jesus as she scolded both of them by saying, 'Lord, tell my sister to get in here and help me.'

But Jesus recognized that she was eating from the wrong tree, and therefore her priorities were way out of order. He answered her,

> *'Martha Martha, you are worried and distracted about many things, but few things are necessary, really only one and Mary **has chosen** the good part.'*

The Kingdom of God is not dos and don'ts

It seems that some people just don't comprehend the nature of God. They can't get a grasp on His love and mercy, so they reduce Him to a rule book, a list of regulations. But thank God for the word through Paul,

> *'For the Kingdom of God is not meat and drink, but **righteousness, peace and joy**.'*　　　　(Romans 14:17)

It is incredible that many people prefer to live by dos and don'ts. It seemingly makes them feel more spiritual. But again, the Gospel is a relationship with a Person, a Person who has fulfilled the law. Truthfully, we are living in a higher realm than dos and don'ts. It is not a set of rules; it is a relationship. St Augustine said, 'Love God and do as you please.' That explains it all. The issue is that we are saved by and in love with a Person, and if we love Him, we can't do as we please. We don't want to break laws, we want to serve Him.

St Francis of Assisi also said it perfectly, 'Preach the Gospel at all times, and if necessary, use words.'

A number of years ago, while praying – well I was actually complaining to the Lord and reminding Him of all my failures and thinking how disappointed He was in me – He interrupted my self-assault. I sat there a few moments, having no expectation that He was going to talk to me. But suddenly I heard His voice with such clarity in my spirit. He said, **'Let's not talk about your report card, let's just fellowship.'** Boy, how that set me free! God is not interested in our failures. He is not interested in death, but life! He speaks from the tree of life, and He offers life. My whole perspective of God changed that day. He doesn't see our relationship with Him as some kind of lifelong score-keeping. He just desires that we enter into the flow of life and enjoy our relationship with Him. Our failures are nothing more than a product of our human nature and we become aware that the flesh profits nothing. It is in the realm of the Spirit where life is produced. He wants us to get caught up in the flow of the Spirit.

'For in Him we live and move and have our being.'
(Acts 17:28)

Every failure should become a stepping stone (not a mountain of condemnation) to launch us into greater spiritual realms.

We never have to be offended

Soon after I was baptized in the Holy Spirit, I became a student at a Christian college. A young man who lived down the hall from me had some religious quirks that frankly turned me off. While home one weekend, I complained about this young man to a lady who had been mentoring me. 'His behavior offends me,' I proclaimed. My mentor answered compassionately but firmly, 'Steve, since you have the Holy Spirit, you never have to be offended by anything.'

I understand now, years later, more than ever what she was saying. We're not to be on the receiving end, but the giving end. Jesus said, 'I didn't come to be ministered to, but to minister.'

If we are filled with the Spirit of God, then we are to be mature and to always be in a position to minister. No longer should we see ourselves as wanting someone to minister to us, but rather to look for opportunities for the Spirit to flow through us. We have the 'upper hand' by the fact that we can recognize we have the living water flowing through us.

> *'Out of his innermost being will flow rivers of living water.'*
> (John 7:39)

We're eating from the tree of life! Therefore our entire purpose of being on the earth is to **give life!**

We don't have to be in bondage by worrying who is ignoring us, talking about us, not understanding us and so forth. We're not on this earth to receive, but to give.

Don't buy in

When people are offended or bitter, they are looking for those who will agree with them and enter into their offense with them. But we must be careful not to 'buy' into their bondage. We must avoid negative relationships, injustices, things that anger or **steal our innocence**. We must **choose** to protect and maintain our state of innocence, by choosing to live from the tree of life and avoid eating from the tree of the knowledge of good and evil.

Therefore, we can love people, but we have to encourage them to choose life, because injustices are everywhere and continually threaten to steal our innocence. The enemy would love us to succumb to anger, hatred, bitterness, resentment, frustration, and any other work of the flesh that produces death. That is why we have to choose ruthlessly to maintain our innocence and eat from the tree of life.

Throw the devil

We can throw the devil and any demons into confusion by refusing to be controlled by the knowledge of good and evil. Therefore, demons are helpless to develop a situation to get us to react to a person who has hurt us or one we cannot forgive. We must adamantly choose life.

A friend of ours was married to an alcoholic, who was miraculously delivered after many years. A few months following his conversion to the Lord and his deliverance from alcohol, a special party was held where he worked. He attended the party and was coerced into taking a drink, and the unfortunate result was he came home inebriated. However, his wife and daughters, although shocked and disappointed by his behavior did not condemn him, but just loved on him instead. They chose to live by the tree of life. He exclaimed later, that it was their attitude that prevented him from jumping back into that lifestyle and losing his victory. He explained that if they had condemned him and spoken harshly to him (the tree of the knowledge of good and evil) he couldn't have handled it at that time in his life and most assuredly it would have driven him back into alcohol abuse. Thank God they choose to live from the tree of life (be wise as serpents and innocent as doves) and offered life and an escape to him, instead of judgment and condemnation. Of course, this is not to say we ignore it when people give in to abuses, we have to take a strong stand. But we must minister life and not death.

Dealing with children

A couple we knew explained their methods of raising their children. Rather than nagging them when they disobeyed, they just insisted that they be responsible or suffer the consequences. For example, their daughter was instructed to do the dishes while they were out for the evening. When they returned home, the dishes were still in the sink, and the daughter was sound asleep in bed, it being well after midnight. They went to her room, turned on the light, and in a tender but firm voice told her she would have to get up and do the dishes. She tried to roll over and go back to sleep, but they insisted she could not until the dishes were completed. They didn't nag her, scold her, or express their extreme disappointment, but simply insisted that she follow through in obedience with what she was told. By nagging her, and judging her as a failure (tree of the knowledge of good and evil) they would have created a permanent condition of 'It's no use, I'm a failure', which would be a death sentence. Instead, they offered her life by simply insisting (without accusing or condemning) that she fulfill her responsibility.

So often, when a child brings home a report card with all As and one B, the parents don't talk about the wonderful job he did by earning As, but rather, 'Why did you get a B?' This ministers death.

One man I know, did this. His son came home with a wonderful report card full of As and Bs. However, the younger daughter came home with Cs and Ds on her report card. He and his wife planned an 'eating out' event – to celebrate the son's grades and to celebrate in advance the improvement that the daughter's grades were **going** to be. She improved! If he had scolded her and intimated she was a failure (the tree of the knowledge of good and evil), she no doubt would have had even more of a decline in her grades and self-esteem.

The 60s

In the 1960s the swelling rebellion in the nation seemed to have two themes, 'If it feels good, do it,' and 'Whatever you do, don't judge anyone.'

This spirit of 'freedom' made some sense to hardened hearts and minds because much of it was aimed at the religious hypocrisy that abounded at that time. The church condemned wrong, but usually from the angle of the tree of the knowledge of good and evil. We saw strange clothing, hair tinted orange or green, long hair on males, and many other eccentricities. Yet few ministered from the tree of life, offering love and acceptance without judgment. Instead, most added fuel to the fire harshly condemning the 'Do your own thing rebellion.' Guilt and condemnation make anyone want to run from God. But everyone wants life, and we can only give life without judging and by remaining in an innocent state.

This was a sadly missed opportunity for the church, solely because few understood how to minister life, instead of condemnation – unable to look beyond the outward appearance and see the needy hearts.

We have to choose between life and death. Choose life!

If you have enjoyed this book and would like to help us to send a copy of it and many other titles to needy pastors in the **Third World**, please write for further information or send your gift to:

Sovereign World Trust
PO Box 777, Tonbridge
Kent TN11 0ZS
United Kingdom

or to the **'Sovereign World'** distributor in your country.

ORDER FORM

Please send me:

_____ copies of ***Those Who Expect Nothing are Never Disappointed – Let My Spirit Move*** ($10.00 each)

_____ copies of ***I Was Always on My Mind*** ($8.00 each)

_____ copies of ***You Can Hear the Voice of God*** ($8.00 each)

_____ copies of ***Breaking the Bondage Barrier – Taking the Limits Off God*** ($7.00 each)

_____ copies of ***You Can't Use Me Today, Lord . . . I Don't Feel Spiritual*** ($6.00 each)

_____ copies of ***Enjoying God and Other Rare Events*** ($4.00 each)

_____ copies of ***Don't Talk to Me Now, Lord . . . I'm Trying to Pray*** ($5.00 each)

_____ copies of ***Listening to the Holy Spirit – Expecting the Miraculous*** ($5.00 each)
[This is a revised edition of *Don't Talk to Me Now, Lord . . . I'm Trying to Pray*]

_____ copies of ***Don't Underestimate the Power of Prayer*** – by Marilyn Sampson ($1.00 each)

_____ copies of ***Medicine for the Mind*** pamphlet (5 for $1.00)

_____ Catalog of cassette tapes

I am enclosing _____ plus $2.00 for postage and handling. (Overseas orders please add an additional 20% of total.)

Mr./Mrs./Miss . . . .

Address . . . .

City, State Zipcode . . . .

Country . . . .

Order from:
Steve Sampson, P.O. Box 36324
Birmingham, Alabama 35236, USA